THE
Million-Dollar
IDEA
IN EVERYONE

WITHDRAWN

W9-BWQ-233

WITHDRAWN

THE Million-Dollar IDEA IN EVERYONE

Easy New Ways to Make Money
from Your Interests, Insights,
and Inventions

MIKE COLLINS

WILEY

John Wiley & Sons, Inc.

ACC LIBRARY SERVICES
AUSTIN, TX

Copyright © 2008 by Michael Collins. All rights reserved.

Published by John Wiley & Sons, Inc., Hoboken, New Jersey.
Published simultaneously in Canada.

No part of this publication may be reproduced, stored in a retrieval system, or transmitted
in any form or by any means, electronic, mechanical, photocopying, recording, scanning,
or otherwise, except as permitted under Section 107 or 108 of the 1976 United States
Copyright Act, without either the prior written permission of the Publisher, or authorization
through payment of the appropriate per-copy fee to the Copyright Clearance Center, Inc.,
222 Rosewood Drive, Danvers, MA 01923, (978) 750-8400, fax (978) 646-8600, or on the
web at www.copyright.com. Requests to the Publisher for permission should be addressed
to the Permissions Department, John Wiley & Sons, Inc., 111 River Street, Hoboken, NJ
07030, (201) 748-6011, fax (201) 748-6008, or online at http://www.wiley.com/go/
permissions.

Limit of Liability/Disclaimer of Warranty: While the publisher and author have used their
best efforts in preparing this book, they make no representations or warranties with respect
to the accuracy or completeness of the contents of this book and specifically disclaim any
implied warranties of merchantability or fitness for a particular purpose. No warranty may
be created or extended by sales representatives or written sales materials. The advice and
strategies contained herein may not be suitable for your situation. You should consult with a
professional where appropriate. Neither the publisher nor author shall be liable for any loss
of profit or any other commercial damages, including but not limited to special, incidental,
consequential, or other damages.

For general information on our other products and services or for technical support, please
contact our Customer Care Department within the United States at (800) 762-2974, outside
the United States at (317) 572-3993 or fax (317) 572-4002.

Wiley also publishes its books in a variety of electronic formats. Some content that appears
in print may not be available in electronic books. For more information about Wiley
products, visit our web site at www.wiley.com.

Designations used by companies to distinguish their products are often claimed by
trademarks. In all instances where the author or publisher is aware of a claim, the product
names appear in Initial Capital letters. Readers, however, should contact the appropriate
companies for more complete information regarding trademarks and registration.

Library of Congress Cataloging-in-Publication Data:

Collins, Mike, 1963–
    The million-dollar idea in everyone: easy new ways to make money from your interests,
insights, and inventions / Mike Collins.
        p. cm.
    Includes bibliographical references and index.
    ISBN 978-0-470-19336-5 (pbk.)
  1. New business enterprises—Management. 2. Home–based businesses—Management.
3. Small business—Management 4. Entrepreneurship. 5. Creative ability in business.
I. Title. II. Title: Ways to make money from your interests, insights, and inventions.

HD62.5.C638 2008
658.1'1412—dc22   2007052395

Printed in the United States of America.

10 9 8 7 6 5 4 3 2 1
ACC LIBRARY SERVICES
AUSTIN, TX

CONTENTS

ACKNOWLEDGMENTS

I would be remiss if I did not pay tribute to a longtime friend and mentor, Harvard Business School professor Clayton Christensen. Most of what I think about innovation comes from studying his research and from our conversations. Clay is a robust academic thinker and one of the greatest minds ever to write about innovation. If you are looking to learn more about innovation, I strongly suggest you read and study his work, such as *The Innovator's Dilemma* (1997), *The Innovator's Solution* (2003), and *Seeing What's Next* (2004). I would also like to thank Shelley Hunter, my partner on this project. Simply put: no Shelley— no book.

T his book describes how we are moving into a world of open innovation where everyday experts like you are making money from life experiences and personal interests. No longer subject to the old rules that mandate years of schooling or climbing your way up a corporate ladder in order to earn a paycheck or to influence an industry, we have entered the era of the amateur where anybody with an Internet connection and a few minutes can turn an interest, insight, or invention into money. You can do this in a small way by taking part in another company's innovative effort, or you can put more into it and start creating opportunities of your own. New ways of participating in the economy are unfolding, and you can either wade into the waters of open innovation or do a big cannonball in the deep end, making a bigger splash (and maybe lots of cash!).

I know this to be true because my professional life is focused on identifying and creating new products and services using open innovation principles. Through my company, Big Idea Group (BIG), I have worked with large corporations as well as with thousands of individuals. And I have seen both groups prosper in this new environment where the walls are down, the mind-set is changed, outsiders' ideas are valued, and individual innovations can be worth millions.

Many smart companies are now offering everyone the chance to be part of an open innovation process: to submit product ideas, share their creativity, influence the types of products and services offered—and be compensated for their input. This goes far beyond traditional focus groups, surveys, and suggestion boxes. At BIG, for example, we have helped clients like Staples, Kraft, Avon, Unilever, and Thomson (to name-drop a few) develop over 60 new products and services, many of which started as ideas from parents, schoolteachers, construction workers, college students, teenagers, and an array of everyday experts who never once set foot in the client's R&D laboratory.

But the open innovation trend is broader than just companies seeking inventive new products. New user-driven businesses like Threadless, Helium, Greeting Card Universe, OurStage, and Can Stock Photo allow anybody to create content and showcase their talents in order to gain recognition and to make money in environments that have been traditionally off-limits. Contributors to these businesses can make anywhere from a couple of dollars to a comfortable living depending on their talent, persistence, and goals. Some participate simply as a creative outlet, while others contribute strategically as part of a more traditional career plan.

For those who want to pursue an open source career more aggressively, the opportunities have never been better. The barriers are continually dropping for everyday experts to participate in and even influence worldwide markets. Entrepreneurship used to be a life-changing commitment that involved raising venture capital, developing a top-notch business plan, and focusing 100 percent of your time and energy on the undertaking. Not anymore. You have more potential for financial solvency as a business owner if you pick a unique area of interest, skip the business plan, and just take one experimental step at a time toward building a new career that will eventually enable you to quit your day job.

As the opportunities to participate in the open source economy increase, so do the communication technologies that make it easier than ever for individuals to create their own venues for reward. Although we talk in this book about a variety of those mediums, like blogs, podcasts, and vodcasts, as well as web sites like Blogger, WordPress, YouTube, MySpace, Facebook, Meetup, Squidoo, and so forth, this is not a how-to book. When you are ready to take advantage of those technologies, review the "Tools, Tips, and Tricks" section of this book (Part Four) to get started, or see if the eighth-grader next door has time to help you out. Bear in mind, however, that these are simply *today's* communication methods. They are likely to be expanded upon long before that neighbor kid graduates from high school.

While the Internet and all of its extended digital and virtual veins are part of what makes open innovation so accessible, using technology is not a requirement. Though having some online presence is preferable, the principles described in this book apply to both everyday experts who plan to travel the information superhighway and those who prefer to take the face-to-face presentation back roads. But while the reality is that anyone can play in this open innovation world, not everybody has figured out how it relates to them, and how they can make money with what they already know. That is where this book comes in.

Having been in the trenches of innovation for the past 20 years as an inventor, inventor agent, venture capitalist, entrepreneur, CEO, and board member, I can help you understand the open innovation environment and find ways to participate. Through my own experiences and by talking with other everyday experts who have managed to succeed in an open innovation environment, I also share tips and suggestions for making your efforts most profitable. So whether you are looking for a part-time income or want to develop an open source career, this book will inspire you to take a chance and make money from the things you already know and love to do.

How I Got My Big Idea

The genesis of Big Idea Group began years ago while I was running a specialty toy company called Kid Galaxy. One of our hottest products, Bendos (a Gumby-like play figure), grossed about $3 million a year and attracted a fair amount of media attention. The exposure increased sales—and brought toy inventors to us in droves. The cold calls and unsolicited product submissions from people hoping to license their inventions were a constant disruption to my already busy days. Of course, I could have barricaded the door and refused to see their products. But amid all the mediocre ideas that landed on my desk, a few cool concepts showed up as well, sparking my interest just enough to allow the invasion to continue.

Although I love innovation—reviewing new products, evaluating potential, figuring out how to make ideas better—the engineer in me grew tired of meeting people in such a random, inefficient way. At the same time, I knew bigger toy companies were facing similar disruptions. So after selling Kid Galaxy, I created BIG to bridge the gap between toy inventors and toy companies.

When I formed BIG, we had a simple plan: Go out and meet with toy inventors, find brilliant inventions, and present a portfolio of products to a toy company in an efficient, organized manner. To get started, I put the word out to inventor communities that I would be conducting BIG invention-review "Roadshows" across the country, looking for toy and game innovations. On my first Roadshow, only about eight people showed up during the entire weekend, and not one idea made it into my A-list portfolio. At the next stop, things were a little better and I met with maybe 15 inventors. But from there, the number of participants steadily increased along with the quality of the products submitted. By the following year, I needed a panel of judges to handle the volume of inventions that arrived, and soon thereafter we expanded our net beyond the toy industry to consumer goods in general.

As BIG's reputation grew among the inventor community, so did our successes in licensing products and simplifying the outside submission process for a variety of clients. Then one day, as I pitched ideas to the CEO of an emerging company, he told me that the products in my portfolio were great, but he really wanted an innovation that addressed a very specific problem. He asked if I could get my inventor network to generate ideas to address that need. That conversation gave rise to the first of many BIG "Idea Hunts," where inventors are given specific requirements (e.g., we need kids' bike accessories that will sell for under five dollars) and the opportunity to license a product with very little investment (rough sketches are accepted, patents are not required). BIG reviews, sifts, and presents the best ideas to the client in a streamlined process so the company receives several innovative ideas created specifically to meet its needs.

BIG evolved again when I met with another CEO who wanted to do an Idea Hunt but could not figure out what problem to have the inventor network solve. That led us to create BIG "Insight Clubs"—private, online consumer communities focused on uncovering opportunities for a client. For example, on behalf of a food company, we might ask 250 parents what their biggest mealtime headaches are. From the responses, we start to see a trend, such as a need for variety packs of pasta sauces or healthy snacks that kids actually like. Insights are collected and given back to clients, who can either work on the solution themselves or put the problem to our inventor network.

So, in response to market demand, my one-man toy-licensing business morphed into an innovation company that facilitates open innovation for even bigger companies. While my work has brought me in contact with many inventors and entrepreneurs, I want to make it clear that you do not need to be an inventor or start a business in order to profit in this world of open innovation. You simply need determination, a little advice from folks working in the area of open innovation, and some inspiration from everyday experts who are already profiting from this exciting trend.

Find out more on: www.TheMillionDollarIdeaInEveryone.com.

PART ONE

GETTING TO KNOW YOU

ONE

Everyday Experts: How People Are Profiting from What They Already Know

When Jim Ruth read an article about an online community that gives aspiring writers the chance to make money and get published, he went to the web site immediately and joined Helium,[1] a user-driven business similar to Wikipedia.[2] With this company, however, contributors are paid for their submissions, given credit for their work, and cannot edit other people's writing. Helium also has a Marketplace where magazines and other publications sponsor writing assignments and will pay for and print the best article submitted.

As an accountant and business consultant often required to write business plans, legal documents, proposals, and so forth, Ruth had a secret desire to write about more entertaining topics and maybe

---

[1]Helium (www.helium.com) is an online writing community where users contribute articles on topics of their choice, get peer review and feedback from other members, can enter writing contests, and can get paid to write articles for publishers through the Helium Marketplace. Peter Tobin, a college student from Cork, Ireland also sold his first article through the Helium Marketplace. Whether you are an aspiring journalist like Tobin or want to test your writing abilities like Ruth did, Helium is a great place to start.

[2]Wikipedia (www.wikipedia.org), a free online encyclopedia, is another user-contributed writing web site, but submissions are anonymous and contributors do not get paid for their work.

even become a freelance writer one day. So he seized the opportunity and started typing.

After writing several pieces on a range of subjects, Ruth scanned the Marketplace for more lucrative assignments and found a request for an article on helping small business owners attract venture capitalists. Since Ruth is well-versed on the art of business funding, he quickly wrote an article and entered it in the contest. Out of several entries, the sponsor selected Ruth's submission, netting him $24 and a byline.

The excitement of being paid for his work and seeing his name in print thrilled Ruth well beyond the few dollars he actually earned. It also inspired him to continue pursuing his freelance writing dream, using Helium to gain exposure and practice his literary skills.

While Ruth is now an everyday expert who writes for Helium and dabbles in open innovation as time permits, others take advantage of the new opportunities to profit from their personal interests more aggressively. After telecommuting for several years, Laura Cunitz started to feel isolated in her home office. So she took a part-time job at a local knitting shop just to meet other people. Cunitz loved the creative environment but soon noticed a disconnect between the way customers and the shop owners approached the knit work process. Customers entered the store thinking about the projects they wanted to make, such as a hat, bag, or sweater. But the store owners only carried items they felt were relevant to their core line of business, such as yarn, needles, and pattern books. That meant knitters often had to visit a variety of retailers to get the other supplies needed to complete a project.

Cunitz felt she could improve this process for knitters, so she walked away from an 18-year marketing career at IBM to open a project-oriented online knitting store called Bella Knitting.[3] Her web site is more than just an online interface to sell knitting projects, however. Cunitz believes that today's knitters are more sophisticated than the stereotypical grandma knitting in a rocking chair, and she also feels strongly that customers should be

---

[3]Bella Knitting can be found online at www.bellaknitting.com.

supported throughout their projects from start to finish. So Bella Knitting provides free online training in the form of instructional content, how-to videos, and a blog that alternates between show-and-tell techniques and the typical ruminations of a daily journal. She draws traffic to Bella Knitting by participating in other heavily trafficked knitting web sites via forums, blogs, and the occasional podcast. Bella Knitting gets hundreds of blog readers a day, and a good portion of those people click over to the web site and buy something.

In fact, business is growing so much that Cunitz often finds herself lacking the time needed to create the imaginative projects her customers have come to expect. So, in a classic case of open innovation, other knitters are invited to submit original ideas to Bella Knitting for licensing through Cunitz's Independent Designer Program. Licensed projects net the contributing designer an initial payment to give Bella Knitting the rights to the pattern, plus a royalty payment for every project sold. Taking advantage of the vast amount of creativity in the knitting community, Cunitz is able to more effectively run her business while increasing the number of projects available to consumers.

Although Cunitz's business background and understanding of technology helped her make the leap from marketing manager to entrepreneur, she certainly did not have a knitting credential or any previous textile industry experience. She just liked to knit, came up with a unique approach to knitting projects, and used open innovation technologies to offer her expertise and services to others.

While Ruth simply tested the open source world by writing a few articles, Cunitz took advantage of open source trends in several different ways. Bypassing traditional methods of selling products and services to consumers, she went directly to consumers by creating an online business, using technology to share her knowledge, participating in social networking to draw others to her expertise, and allowing others to share their creativity in her forum. Both Ruth and Cunitz's experiences, however, are part of the process that provides ways for you to make money doing something you love. Yes, change is hard, and many people cling to the traditional view that you need to write a book, go to a fancy school, have an impressive resume, or have a surplus of cash to make an impact. But thanks to open innovation, that view is evolving: Now we are all experts with the power to profit from our passions and interests.

A ONE-MINUTE HISTORY OF INNOVATION

Since the Industrial Revolution, innovation has been a closed system where a finite group of people, typically working for a corporation, were deemed experts in the market segment they represented. People with years of schooling, industry experience, or credentials profited from their expertise and essentially kept the rest of us out—or very selectively admitted us.

If you wanted to be a television critic, for example, you had to attend the right school, start your career in the mail room, and, with some luck and talent, eventually work your way up to writing for the *New York Times* or *TV Guide*. If you wanted to teach people how to improve their golf backswing, you had to be a golf instructor at a country club. If you wanted a recording contract, you had to play in local bars, hoping to be discovered by a talent scout who might take your demo tape to a couple of suits at a high-profile record label. These are generalizations, of course, but the point is that opportunities to profit from unique skills and abilities were limited; reaching a goal often required a lifetime commitment, and the power to decide whose ideas would be considered rested with a centralized group of people.

In the consumer goods industry, the experts were the guys in lab coats in the research and development department of a major corporation. Working within the confines of a corporate structure where layers of management and committees were involved in every decision, these inventors or old-school experts created products and services they believed consumers needed. Ideas from independent inventors were often disregarded because it was believed that a person working outside the fortress could not possibly have the knowledge needed to teach the experts anything new. But this closed world system often produced only incremental improvements—improved, bigger, lighter, low-fat, low-carb, 30-percent more, and the like—rather than disruptive innovations that made a difference.

The rest of the development team members were almost as narrow in their viewpoint. The marketing group would weave a brand strategy around the product, hold a focus group to tweak the message, spend a few million in advertising, and send the sales group to stores. Only after spending millions of dollars bringing the product to market would the company then discover whether the general public really wanted the latest flavor of Coke.

What forces have changed this paradigm and increased companies' willingness to use the open innovation model? Contributing factors are the failure rate of new products, unprecedented levels of competition for consumer dollars created by the global economy, and Internet competition for traditional brick-and-mortar customers (if you cannot find the product you are looking for at the local drugstore, you can probably find it online). Companies must innovate to survive. Those who recognize the value of getting additional input and ideas from people beyond the walls of their corporate environments simply stand a better chance of competing.

Getting into the Open Innovation Movement

Unlike the old model, where you either worked fully in a given industry ("I am a journalist," "I am a teacher," "I am a plumber," and so forth) or you did not, the open innovation economy is a spectrum where you can decide how hard to play and whether you want to focus on one area in depth or dabble in many. Though there are beginning, intermediate, and advanced levels of play, there is no real hierarchy in terms of your possible gains. In other words, a person taking advantage of beginning innovation opportunities can make just as much (or more) money as a person working on the other end of the spectrum.

The distinguishing characteristics of each level are the amount of time and effort you want to put into the endeavor, the uniqueness of your talents, and the degree of control you want over what interests and passions you pursue. You can be like Ruth and participate a little at a time, taking advantage of opportunities created for you by open innovation companies. Or you can be like Cunitz and work full-time to create a microbusiness (which might become a big business) focused exactly on the passions you want to pursue. Then again, you might want to be somewhere in the middle. The options are as open as the open innovation world itself.

Understanding the investment required and creative control allowed within each level of the spectrum will help you match your expertise and goals with the opportunities that are available.

WHAT IS OPEN INNOVATION?

The concept of open innovation comes from the computer industry and a time when some software companies decided to make their source code (the basic language of a program) available to the people who use it. Previously, the proprietary source code was literally hidden from users because only compiled versions of programs were distributed. By opening the source code for users to see, the sponsoring companies discovered that programmers not only adopted the software more quickly, but they jumped at the opportunity to tinker with the code and collaborate with other users. The user community fed fixes and suggestions back to the developers, resulting in a significantly better product than the original version. Thus the open source code approach benefited both the users and the software company.

Although the terminology started as technical jargon, *open innovation* now generically refers to the notion of allowing outsiders the opportunity to contribute, participate, and profit in a previously closed environment. For example, an ice cream manufacturer that once internally determined what ice cream flavors to put in stores now creates a contest to allow consumers to decide. People submit ideas, the top five entries are listed on a web site for consumers to vote on, and the person who submitted the winning flavor receives a cash prize plus free ice cream for a year. Or, with less drama, that same company might set up an online focus group that allows consumers to give feedback on new ice cream commercials in exchange for free product coupons.

Individuals can participate in open innovation by working with a company or they can create opportunities of their own, bypassing traditional methods of consumer outreach. For example, an inventor might decide to manufacture and sell his product on the Internet rather than license it to a manufacturer or try to sell it wholesale to stores. Another consumer wanting to help people make better buying decisions about baby food could write a blog and participate in web site forums about baby products. A singer wanting to showcase his voice and get people interested in his singing might upload videos of his nightclub appearances to YouTube. With an ever-increasing array of technologies, everyday experts can go straight to the public with whatever it is they have to   share.

Open innovation allows people who previously had limited or zero innovation opportunity the chance to work with companies or create opportunities of their own using the latest technology. And the speed at which that innovation takes place is remarkably quick because the layers of process and middlemen have been reduced significantly. If you have a product to sell, just set up a web site and sell it. Forget the rules. Just get started.

Beginning Level: Test Your Expertise

Investment required: low.

Creative control: low.

At the beginning end of the spectrum, you are taking advantage of opportunities created by other companies rather than creating opportunities of your own. That might mean participating in an open source contest, like submitting a product idea to the Staples Invention Quest or uploading a homemade video to the Doritos Super Bowl commercial challenge. Beginning level participation might also mean contributing content (written articles, photography, cartoons, greeting card designs, etc.) to user-driven businesses where the opportunities to participate are ongoing and more than one person has a chance to win. And when America tires of voting for the next pop star, and crowd-sourcing projects like Helium and Wikipedia become the norm rather than headline news, other ways to contribute to companies are very likely to emerge.

Though the ways in which corporations engage consumers may evolve, the primary benefit of participating at this level is that you decide which businesses to work with and how often you want to contribute. Most important, you do not have to start a business or make a substantial investment to get involved. A secondary benefit is that beginners succeeding at this level often gain confidence in their own expertise ("I guess I really do know what I am talking about") and decide to participate in other open source opportunities or graduate into the more entrepreneurial levels of play with some sense that the additional commitment will be worth the effort.

The downside of dabbling in this level is that you have little control over what opportunities become available. I know more about bar food than snack food, for example, but Welch's Afterschool Snack Idea Hunt is looking for the latter, so I would need to align my creativity with their requirements in order to make a potentially profitable contribution. And though I will probably never be able to come up with a decent entry for the Steve Madden Art and Sole Shoe Contest, I am well qualified to submit ideas for things involving baseball, craps, and the iPhone should the opportunity to do so arise.

In Chapter 5, we take you through the beginning level of open innovation and teach you how to be profitable in that environment. You may decide to stay and play for as long as your life experiences, skills, and interests match up with the opportunities available. But if you succeed at that level and want to leverage your good fortune, or if you have unique expertise you would like to exploit on your own, then taking a small step up to the intermediate level is the best way to increase your enterprising commitment without taking on too much risk.

Intermediate Level: Find Your Sweet Spot

Investment required: medium.

Creative control: high.

Unlike the beginning level, where corporations tell you what talents and insights to share, at the intermediate level you become more entrepreneurial and *you* decide what everyday expertise to share with the world. To prosper at this level, however, you need to be rather specific about your talents and interests. For example, while just being a mom who makes dinner for her kids might be enough to get paid for your opinions at the beginning level of innovation,[4] the intermediate route would require you to identify some unique aspect of that role in order to create a niche for yourself. So you need to think of the attributes that make you unique. What life experiences have you had? What do you know how to do? Where have you been, who have you met, and what do you know?

No need to answer these questions right now. In Chapter 4, we take you through a personal inventory to help you figure out several areas of expertise to explore. We also talk about how to narrow and combine general interests in order to derive specialties. In later

---

[4]You can learn more about the Big Idea Group Insight Clubs by selecting "Insight Clubs" on our web site at www.bigideagroup.net. If you want to go directly to the Insight Clubs and register, you can do that at www.bigideaclubs.net.

chapters, we talk about ways in which you can demonstrate your expertise, gain exposure for the things you know, and earn credibility that can be used to make money or provide a springboard to either traditional job opportunities or the advanced levels of open innovation.

At the intermediate level, there is still no need to (and please do *not*) give up your day job. Instead, you will spend your time building a platform (a voice, a brand, a consistent message) that uniquely describes you, your abilities, and what it is you can offer people. You can build that platform working part-time with relatively little investment. Doing so will help you adapt to customer reaction and test the market of your idea before making any real investment. Only when the platform is stabilized and you are experiencing success on some level should you consider moving to the advanced level of open innovation, where the investment is higher and the potential to make money increases.

Advanced Level: Kick It Up a Notch

Investment required: high.

Creative control: high.

In the old, closed innovation world, you had to make a significant investment of time and money in order to create a business doing what you love. But in the world of open innovation, you do not start at this advanced level. The process is much more evolutionary. Rather than quitting your job and taking on investors in order to open a business, you ease into starting a full-time company by first creating a foundation and testing the market at the intermediate level. Only when that foundation proves successful should you jump to this advanced stage, knowing that the endeavor has the potential to be even more successful and profitable with your concentrated effort.

There are so many ways in which to participate in open innovation that the decision of how you will make money comes down to picking the expertise you would like to exploit in conjunction with the resources you want to spend. While the beginning level of innovation tends to favor creative contributions—product ideas, designs, photography, and so forth—in the intermediate and advanced stages, more strategic thinking will prevail. So if you are a talented, creative person, you could remain at the beginning level, hopping from one opportunity to the next, and make a very nice income. However, if you have a burning desire to do something in particular—teach people how to install tile or demonstrate your expertise in line dancing—you will need to work a little harder to attract people in order to showcase your talents. But it can be done.

Ten years ago, it would have been impossible to reach people with so little effort and to interact with people across town, let alone the globe. But the new environment is open, and we are on the tip of the technologies that make it easier than ever to be entrepreneurial.

Whether you want to dabble in the world of open innovation to save for a vacation or start a microbusiness to make a life change, there are a number of ways in which you can make money in the open source movement. Though we talk about those opportunities in detail throughout this book, keep in mind that open innovation is an evolving story. We lay a framework of beginning, intermediate, and advanced opportunities, but the ways in which to participate at each level may change over time. And while the examples I give in this book are exciting and empowering for the everyday expert, they are just today's examples. I believe we are at the start of the open innovation trend, where exciting new tools and ways to play are continually appearing.

INNOVATION IS NOT JUST INVENTING

Innovation is the creation of something new that solves a problem. Although an invention certainly fits that description, innovation is more than just creating a new gizmo. Innovation can be a new process, service, mind-set, concept, message, or strategy that is better than the existing alternatives.

Red Bull Energy Drink is an example of innovation, but not because the liquid inside the can is anything special. The drink is innovative because the makers of Red Bull were the first to promote the caffeine content and other energy-boosting ingredients in their beverage as a way to help people become mentally more alert or physically more awake. Prior to Red Bull, consumers who wanted a carbonated beverage to overcome fatigue (a commuter driving home after a long day at work, a student pulling an all-nighter to write a term paper, college kids going clubbing, etc.) often chose Mountain Dew— a brand that actually downplayed its caffeine levels. Red Bull's innovative market position created the carbonated energy drink category.

Innovation can be a service. Stephanie Allen, a caterer and working mom, struggled to put healthy meals on the table for her family at dinnertime. To solve the problem, she started making a month's worth of meals ahead of time and freezing the dinners for her family to use on busy weeknights. When friends caught on to her method, they asked if she would help them do the same thing for their families. So Allen and a friend, Tina Kuna, rented out a catering facility and invited 20 women to participate in a meal-making session that ultimately spurred the creation of Dream Dinners, the first of many retail meal-assembly kitchens.*

Before Dream Dinners, the primary alternative to premaking home-cooked meals for a family would be to actually prepare the meals at home—a luxury many time-crunched people cannot afford. Now busy moms can schedule an appointment at Dream Dinners, choose meals from a menu of options, bring along friends to make the evening more like a party, and leave with several healthy meals ready to freeze. In starting this service business, not only did Allen and Kuna turn their dinner-making idea into a profitable venture, but they became the originators of the meal-assembly industry.

*Although a variety of other meal-assembly stores have since opened up around the country, Dream Dinners (www.dreamdinners.com) was the first.

Innovation can also be a strategy. Pottery Barn furniture store teamed up with paint manufacturer Benjamin Moore & Company to create a unique palette of paint colors designed to perfectly complement the furniture sold at Pottery Barn. The name and number of the Benjamin Moore paints are prominently displayed throughout Pottery Barn's catalog, web site, and retail stores—taking the guesswork out of paint selection for Pottery Barn customers. Now Benjamin Moore is also selling paint samples at kiosks strategically located right outside Pottery Barn stores in the mall. Selling paint right next to the stores where consumers who are likely to need the paint will be shopping (versus the hardware store) is an innovative strategy.

Personal branding—the concept of using your skills and expertise to establish a unique and profitable platform—is innovation. Rachael Ray, for example, is not just another cook with a fun personality. She created a concept called "30-Minute Meals" and parlayed that platform into cookbooks, cooking shows, a daytime television talk show, a magazine, and seemingly endless endorsement deals. Though Ray used the 30-minute concept to become a widely known cooking expert, her name brand is seemingly on everything from cooking supplies to Wheat Thins. The concept of personal branding is an innovation, and the people who manage to pull it off are innovators.

And finally, yes, inventions can also be innovations. The first MP3 device invented to store, organize, and play digital music is an innovation. The Apple iPod itself, though beautifully designed, was initially called just another MP3 player. But coupling the iPod player with a method of legally downloading digital music, via the iTunes online music library, and a host of tightly bound applications that make all music easily portable, is an innovation in terms of both the technology and the lifestyle impact the product has made on an enormous segment of the population. Products can be innovative, but innovation is not limited to just products.

Think Big, Start Small

One of the main themes of this book is that you can make money doing what you love by taking one small step at a time. Rather than drawing from your retirement account to open a restaurant or take on some other large-scale, full-time business, you can and should start small, let the market dictate your moves, and gradually increase the amount of time and money you invest as opportunities present themselves. In doing so, you are more likely to be receptive to changes in what you thought would work versus what is actually working, and what you thought you wanted to do versus what you actually enjoy doing.

When I started the Kid Galaxy toy company, for example, I had just left the Pleasant Company, makers of the hugely successful American Girl Doll collection. I wanted to build on what I had learned and create something similar in price and quality for boys. So my team and I came up with the concept of making large, wooden vehicles like trucks, tanks, and fire engines. After developing a few prototypes, we set up a photo shoot to take pictures of young children playing with the toys. But the kids were totally disinterested in the products, and the pictures were boring. As a team, we huddled together to chart our next move.

Not quite ready to scrap the wooden toys yet, we came up with the idea to add plastic, bendable characters to the product line. After making a few prototypes of truck drivers, firemen, and so forth, we brought the kids back into the studio for more pictures. This time the kids went nuts. But they could not have cared less about the wooden vehicles. They only played with the Gumby-like guys sitting in them. That day, I told the Kid Galaxy team we were dumping the trucks to make 24 different bendable characters, which we eventually called Bendos.

Since our only real investment at that point had been developing prototypes, we easily switched directions when the customers clearly demonstrated what they did and did not want from us. In one afternoon, Kid Galaxy transitioned from a manufacturer of high-end wooden toys to a maker of lower-priced, flexible characters that ultimately netted the company several million dollars in revenue.

I also learned during my time at the helm of Kid Galaxy that the real high for me is the innovation stage of product development—coming up with the next big idea, recognizing good ideas from others, and then turning those concepts into marketable products. So when the Bendos craze began to sunset, I sold the company and started BIG, where I could focus full-time on the area in which I am most passionate.

Myself included, most entrepreneurs who ultimately succeed in creating a profitable business doing something they love get there after the initial strategy and even plan B get derailed. In fact, plan F or G is more likely to be the winning approach. The beginning stage of any new venture is a time for experimentation, both for you and for the business. Therefore, whether you decide to participate in open innovation by entering contests as time permits or are planning to create a full-time business allowing you to quit your current career, craft a dream scenario for yourself, but let the process of getting there be evolutionary.

Thinking Big

Big is relative. For some people, thinking big means wanting to own a company that makes several million dollars and employs a hundred people. For others, it means having the freedom to work from home so they can coach a Little League team without asking for time off. And for some it means earning a few hundred extra dollars a month so they can take family vacations without using credit cards. Whatever your goals are, the first aspect of thinking big is creating a visual image of what you hope to achieve.

The details are important, so allow yourself to daydream a bit. What would you be doing? What would your day be like? Where would you be working and what kind of people would be sitting alongside you? When you figure out what you want to be doing and how you want to be doing it, make that vision your North Star. Use it to motivate you to get started and overcome the rejections and disappointments that are inevitable whenever you start a new venture. More important, pointing your mental telescope toward your ultimate goal can guide you in making all of the microdecisions you will need to make in order to reach your North Star. That does not mean you will not make mistakes. But having a sense of where you want to go will help you take advantage of opportunities that put you in line with your North Star and avoid those that do not. The North Star can also provide the extra push we all need from time to time to do the work of turning dreams into realities.

Though you should start the journey with small steps, a big-picture focus will help ensure that the initial groundwork you do will support your long-term objectives. Suppose, for example, you want to be an everyday expert on hamster care so that you can eventually start a hamster rescue organization. Taking small steps toward that goal, you might first create a free blog on WordPress.com to publish some of the information you already know.[1] Since your three hamsters have more toys in their Habitrail than most kids have in their playroom, the first few posts you plan to write will be about

---

[1] *Blog* is short for *Web log*. Blogs are similar to regular web sites except there is a page (an area on the web site) where you can easily make frequent entries. If you have an e-mail address and about 30 seconds, you can set up a free blog on Wordpress.com (www .wordpress.com). If you request the username "HamsterKingdom," for example, your blog address will be www.hamsterkingdom.wordpress.com. If you prefer a personalized domain name (like www.hamsterkingdom.com), you can register it with Wordpress.com for a few dollars. You do not have to pay for additional web hosting services because the blog is already hosted by WordPress. Another nice thing about this service is that if you decide later to upgrade your web site to a more robust, customized site, you can use Wordpress.org and all your original pages, content, and links will transfer seamlessly.

hamster toys—the best and the worst, safety issues, and cleaning procedures. Though initially you plan only to discuss the light-hearted topics you are most familiar with, the business foundation you create (web site address, business name, and so on) should reflect your bigger goal. For example, rather than creating a blog called Hamster Toys, your name of choice should be far more encompassing, such as Hamster Haven, a name that represents your current topics as well as the more important ones you plan eventually to cover.

The second aspect of thinking big is acting big. I talk to people all the time who do not think they know enough about a particular topic to be considered an everyday expert. So they wait, thinking they need to take just one more class, read one more book on the topic, or have someone else give them the go-ahead to put themselves out there. And when they do finally feel comfortable sharing what they know, they do it with far too much humility. You are more likely to be taken seriously as an everyday expert if you act confident right from the start and always project yourself to be where you are going rather than where you currently are. In doing so, not only will you establish credibility faster, but you will actually pull yourself in the direction you want to go. Though you must always intend to fulfill the promises you make ("All Things Hamster!"), you do not need to know everything the day you begin.

The third aspect of thinking big is balancing those big thoughts with little action steps. The worst thing you can do is spend the bulk of your time developing an elaborate business plan that will take lots of time to write and require a ton of money to execute. That strategy works maybe once in a million times. I think you can have that ambition, but you are far better off spending a little bit of time planning and a lot more time experimenting and taking steps to reach your North Star. In developing a new product, for example, you can talk all day long about how it will work, who will buy it, and how much money you can make. But only when you start picking out the cardboard and tape to make the prototype or asking people if they like your idea do you really start to learn and take steps toward turning your idea into a reality. Though you must always think big in order to achieve big dreams, you will save time and money if you start with small, incremental steps.

Starting Small

One of the biggest mistakes I see people make is solidifying their innovations too soon. Instead, you should think of your potential new business the way a scientist would: Have an idea, write down some assumptions, create a clever way to test the assumptions (remember, no money!), and be open to the possibility that the assumption might be wrong. As human beings, we change, we learn, and we grow. Your original goal of working from home may leave you feeling isolated instead of independent. The vision of spending all your time talking about hamsters may make you feel like you are running on a gerbil wheel yourself. Or the number of people you thought wanted to know about the things you have to share might not be that large a population after all. Keep your time and financial investments very modest in the beginning so you can experiment and change directions if your North Star moves.

Although I have built several successful companies in my entrepreneurial life, I started each one taking the same baby steps. The first thing I do is create a physical workspace and set my office hours. That routine of getting up in the morning, showering, and going to the office, whatever and wherever that office may be, helps me treat the new venture as a job. When I started BIG, for example, I went to Home Depot and bought two file cabinets and a plain door to make a desk. Then I rented an 8 × 8 foot, windowless office for a few hundred dollars a month, set up my door-desk, and started cold-calling potential clients.

For me, the workspace needs to be outside of my home to help separate those two aspects of my life, but that may not be the case for you. Your workspace can be an attic, a basement, or part of a bedroom. It can even be a shared space, like the family's computer room, or just a box of notes and file folders you put on the kitchen table whenever you get a chance to work. Where your workspace is does not matter. The important thing is that you have one.

I am a big believer in treating the business of starting a business like a job itself. For me, it works best to jump in full-time. Again, you have to find something that works for you and your goals. Your time allotment could be as little as 30 minutes a day or just Thursday nights when your wife is at bingo. Do not let the inability to spend a great deal of time, however, be an excuse for not spending any time at all. In less than 10 minutes, you could set up a web site on Yahoo,[2] create a MySpace account,[3] or post a few comments to a user forum, and literally be one step closer to reaching your ultimate destination.

The second thing I do is create an inexpensive identity. Establishing a presence is as much a psychological step as it is a physical one. Thinking of a company name, crafting a slogan, developing a sales pitch, and so forth, are all steps that make the vision of what I am trying to do come into focus. It also helps me to communicate my objectives to others. If they cannot clearly understand what I am trying to accomplish, then I know more refinement is required.

Of course, you do not have to spend thousands of dollars hiring a graphic artist to design a logo, build a custom web site, or get expensive business cards and letterhead printed up. Instead, use inexpensive technology like Blogger (free web site)[4] and VistaPrint

---

[2]A variety of services allow you to create a free web site. Most free sites, however, include their service name in your Web address. With Yahoo! GeoCities, for example, you can create a free web site but your desired name will be imbedded in its site name (such as www.geocities.hamsterkingdom.com). I recommend you spend a few extra bucks now and create your own domain name, because it will be easier to grow your business if your web address does not change in the process. Regardless of the domain name you choose, the benefit of using free web site services is that you can create Web pages quickly using a variety of templates, and the investment is minimal if things do not work out as hoped.

[3]If you think MySpace (www.MySpace.com) is just for teenagers, think again. Many enterprising people are using free MySpace accounts to quickly get online and advertise, test-market, and sell their wares. It might not be the best venue for promoting a commercial real estate business, but it is perfectly suited for promoting things like Hot Picks Guitar Picks (at www.myspace.com/hotpicksusa). On this site, fans can see the picks, read testimonials, give their opinion on upcoming designs, participate in a user community, and so forth. To buy a pick, users simply click a banner advertisement that will redirect them to the Hot Picks home page at www.hotpicksusa.com. The Hot Picks MySpace site is a great example of using a social networking site to increase interest and draw traffic to a traditional web site.

[4]Blogger (www.blogger.com) is another place where you can set up a free Web log.

(free business cards)[5] to get the business up and running quickly. Save the investment of creating a customized image for when you have proven the business and know the money spent will be worth it.

Third, to avoid feeling overwhelmed, I break daunting tasks into smaller, manageable ones. One technique I use is to start and end each work session with a list. For the first five minutes, I jot down small tasks I can finish during that time frame. At the end of the session, I write down one thing I want to complete the next day. Thus, I never start off staring at a blank piece of paper.

And instead of writing vague chores such as "Become a stock photographer," I break hefty items down into smaller, more achievable goals like "Research microstock photography Web sites,"[6] "Write down photo quality requirements," "Ask question in user forum about which camera to buy," "Submit 5 to 10 photos," and so forth. Although, in the early stages, your list may contain several education items, always balance the learning with the action so you are quickly inching your way closer to your goals.

And last, because it can be so easy to get caught up in the day-to-day tactical world of lists and blogs and business cards, I routinely force myself to pull back and check the alignment to my North Star vision. Though I do this throughout all aspects of running a business, I do it more often in the early stages. Whenever I try a new market or try selling my services in a new way, I think of the activity as an experiment and check my alignment again. Some of the steps I take will be right and others will be wrong, but I do not see either as a failure. I see the activity as an opportunity to learn more about my potential business and about myself.

---

[5]VistaPrint (www.vistaprint.com) offers free business cards as long as you select one of the free designs, pay for shipping, and agree to have the VistaPrint logo printed on the back of the cards. You can, however, upgrade to a customized design relatively inexpensively.

[6]Microstock photography web sites like Can Stock Photo (www.canstockphoto.com), Shutterstock (www.shutterstock.com), and iStockphoto (www.istockphoto.com) are repositories of hundreds of thousands of quality photographs that anybody can purchase and download for use. Typical customers are Web designers, graphic artists, magazines, and other creatives who would rather pay to use existing artwork than hire a photographer to set up a costly photo shoot. Anybody can contribute pictures to a stock photography web site. Contributors get paid when their photos are selected for use.

OTHER EVERYDAY EXPERTS TALK ABOUT GETTING STARTED

Eric Teng, Inventor of the Garlic Twist[*]

Be reasonable in evaluating your ideas, what your skills are, and how much risk you can afford to take. Make sure there is a market and thus commercial value for your invention before investing in it. Whacky products may qualify for a patent but may not be good for anything else. I have seen inventors spend tons of money on products that only the inventor loves, and that is not a sensible approach. The process of inventing a product demands considerable resources so it is not something to be taken lightly. If you do not have the financial backing to start a project full-time, keep your day job and begin the process slowly.

Julie Savage, Ideas to Grow, Inventor and Insight Club Participant[†]

Set aside your fear of rejection. Many people have wonderful ideas that they never pursue because of lack of time or lack of belief that anything will ever come of it. If you set the idea aside, for sure nothing will happen. But you really have nothing to lose by trying.

---

[*]Eric Teng started working on the Garlic Twist (www.garlictwist.com) when he got frustrated with a traditional garlic press and envisioned a two-piece device that would rub or twist together to magically peel and mince a clove of garlic. After several failed prototypes, he realized two opposing rows of cross-cutting teeth were needed to dice the garlic and keep it in place so the user could repeat the process for smaller bits if desired.

[†]Julie Savage likes to invent products and teach her children how to invent as part of their homeschooling curriculum. She has won several contests and her children have also been finalists in a variety of inventing contests, including the Staples Invention Quest Kids contest. You can see her portfolio of awards on www.ideastogrow.com.

Shannon Kaye, Decorative Painter and Host of *Fresh Coat*[*]

Let your work and knowledge speak for itself, and resist the urge to downplay your talents, point out flaws that only you can see, or diminish your expertise simply because it came by way of life experience rather than education or special training. When I look back at all the jobs I have had and the lessons I have learned, my seemingly crooked resume now appears to be a straight path of diverse skills I needed to gather in order to be successful in pursuing the work that I love. If you, too, follow your instincts and pursue your passions, you are sure to wind up where you belong as well.

Susan Kern, Creator of Tiny Totes[†]

As an innovator, you may hear "no" 99 times for every one yes, but do not take the rejection personally. Instead, listen to the comments of people who have been in the industry longer than you have, and see if your idea can be improved based on their feedback. If you know something is good, you can find a home for it. But also be willing to dump an idea and move on. Some people have a hard time letting go when they have tunnel vision for a single idea. When I have a product that I believe in, I take advice from others, revise, and reinvent until I have something that is working and overcomes previous objections. If I cannot make that happen, then the idea goes back in the box and I try something else.

[*] Shannon Kaye is the host and designer of the television show *Fresh Coat* on the DIY Network. She has also written a book called *Fresh Coat*, in which she gives detailed how-to instructions for some of the projects featured on her show. Though Kaye has had much success, she is mostly a self-taught artist with do-it-yourself roots. Her web site is www.shannonkaye.com.

[†] Susan Kern is a habitual inventor. She licensed a children's toy called Tiny Totes to the Basic Fun Toy Company and is always coming up with new ideas.

Pursue Your Passion, Let the Money Follow

I t is six o'clock on a Monday morning and the alarm just went off. Another long work week lies ahead of you and it is time to get out of bed and face it. Are you ready to embrace the day? Or does the thought of going back to the grind make you swear under your breath as you get in the shower, or fantasize about winning the lottery so you can quit this stupid routine?

We all get the occasional Monday morning blues after a nice weekend or a long vacation. But if Monday morning dread plays out in your mind every single week, then you should probably be doing something different. I am not telling you to quit your job today, however. Instead, start putting effort toward the goal of doing something you are passionate about so that one day you can pop out of bed on a Monday ready to tackle the week's challenges. It really is possible.

I love what I do. I meet interesting and creative people, evaluate their inventions and business ideas, learn what big businesses are working on, and explore opportunities where I can bring parties together in a way where everybody makes money. I love seeing innovative ideas work—and learning from those that do not. I am endlessly amazed by interesting people and I meet an everyday expert each time I talk with someone new.

While I love my job in a general sense, I certainly do not love every moment of running a company. I do not relish a day when I have to handle a tough human resource issue or work my way out from under paperwork that piled up while I was on a business trip. But the passion I feel for my work carries me through the lackluster tasks and difficult times I have to face.

If you are not passionate about your job, then every aspect of it feels like work and every disappointment is a new reason to think about quitting. But if you love what you are doing for a living, then the majority of the things you do each day will be satisfying and invigorating. As you embark on a quest to make money doing something you love, know that the road will not be without bumps. Every business has challenges. The trick is to find out what types of challenges you enjoy and which ones drain you.

Going outside of traditional career paths takes courage and persistence. Although I lay out a framework here, your everyday expertise is unique to you. Ultimately, you will have to figure out how to adapt these guidelines to the things you love to do. Money is not guaranteed to follow. But if you patiently and persistently work through the adversity that awaits you, the money is likely to be there. Regardless, I promise you that the journey will have been worth the effort.

PASSION CHOOSES YOU

Although I talk at length in this book about having the courage to follow your passion for a particular hobby or interest, there are times when the subject of your everyday expertise chooses you. You may be faced with a particular life experience such as having someone in your family affected by a disease. Or you may be dealing with an unusual circumstance such as bees nesting in your house or ladybugs infesting your kitchen. Or maybe you have just been thrust into a position you did not ask for, such as chairing the school fundraising committee, simply because nobody else made eye contact when they were looking for a volunteer.

Whatever the reason, you rose to the challenge and now have a wealth of knowledge and life experience to share with others. You may not have chosen to become an expert in this field, but you are passionate about it now. So whether you decide to share your insight with the world as a service or as a way to make a living, use the open innovation technologies to reach as many people as possible so when someone new is faced with a similar challenge, they will have you to turn to.

Be Patient and Persistent

At one point in my life, I pursued photography as a hobby. But after about six months, I realized I did not have the talent for it, nor did I want to spend any time improving my skills. I liked taking pictures, but I did not have what I would consider *passion* for photography. So I set the camera aside and moved on to other interests.

If you are passionate about something, you make time for it. Giving it up is not an option. And although improving your skills or expanding upon what you already know may not always be easy, you are driven to do it anyway. You devote all your spare mental cycles to thinking about spending more time pursuing this particular hobby or interest, and you imagine getting to spend your days following your heart instead of a paycheck.

You need that kind of passion to become an everyday expert because making money doing something you enjoy will ultimately require some effort. You can dabble for fun and you can earn side money putting in just a couple of hours a week. But if you truly want to support yourself through open innovation principles, you will have to put in a significant amount of time and energy. You also need to be patient.

Starting a new business takes time. Getting profitable takes even more time. But follow my advice and start slowly. Figure out what you really want to do and what you are really good at. Experiment. Make mistakes. Learn from those mistakes. Test yourself and the market and do not—repeat, *do not*—quit your job until one of those career experiments takes root, consumers respond favorably to one of your ideas, or some other exciting opportunity unveils itself. Although the media makes it appear as though overnight success is happening all around, it really is not. We just do not hear about the J. K. Rowling and Google-type sensations until after they have earned their success and they are suddenly profiled in every newspaper and magazine on the planet.

Though the subjects of those success stories seem to have come from nowhere, typically they have been slowly and steadily plodding along in the background, pursuing their hobbies and interests, refining their skills, working late nights, and persevering through disappointments in order to reach their North Stars. The people I know who are successful entrepreneurs do just that. They know what they value and what they want in life. Then they steadily and consistently work toward achieving those goals over years, if not decades.

You might be tempted to shortcut the process and quit your job so you can quickly get on with the business of doing what you love. That is a bit like joining a seminary because the girl dumps you. Taking that approach will create stress and lead to poor decision making, wasted money, and operating in panic mode. The bills will start piling up, the credit cards will reach their limits, and you will be peddling as fast as you can just to get the business operational. Forget profitability in that case. And forget about being able to change directions as you experiment, because you will be too far invested at that point to change your mind.

The patient approach may take longer in the beginning because you are giving yourself the freedom to explore, experiment, and fail. But once you arrive at that magical crossroad where your passionate interest intersects with positive consumer reaction, open innovation technologies can help you become a recognizable everyday expert at an astounding rate.

If you have always wanted to write a children's book, then write it. You do not have to wait for a publisher to buy the rights—you can self-publish the book and start selling it on a web site or make it available on Amazon.com.[1] If you want to make money fixing computers, hang a flier outside of coffee shops that offer free wireless Internet access and post an advertisement on Craigslist.[2] If you have a song to sing, then sing it. Record it yourself, and put it up on YouTube for others to see.

You may spend years learning a craft and a few more months trying to figure out how to offer your expertise in a way that gives you satisfaction and extra income, but patience and persistence during that time will help you reach your ultimate goal of making money doing something you love. If you are not passionate about what it is you want to do, it will be too tempting to quit when the business of doing what you love requires time and effort.

PLANNING FOR YOUR FUTURE

Having a job used to mean having stability, good benefits, and a place to work until you retired comfortably. You got pay increases that made a small difference to your lifestyle, and "cutting costs" meant the year-end bonuses would be slightly less than the year before. But the employment world has changed. Few companies offer job stability, cutting costs

[1]Self-publishing is becoming an easy way for authors to see their writing in print without having to wait for a publishing house to buy it. Some people make enough money through the sale of their self-published books to happily continue writing and working in that way. Others use the success of a self-published book to attract a traditional publishing contract. To learn more about self-publishing, check out a prominent print-on-demand web site called BookLocker (www.booklocker.com).

Amazon.com also offers print-on-demand services for books, CDs, DVDs, and other media. You do not have to use their services, however, to sell your products on Amazon. To learn more, go to www.amazon.com, select "Help" from the main menu, and then select "Publisher & Vendor Guides" from the menu on the left-hand side.

[2]Craigslist (www.craigslist.com) is a great way to sell an old desk or find a deal on firewood, but you can also use it to let people know about your everyday expertise. On Joan Stewart's web site (www.thepublicityhound.com), you can buy a CD or download a transcript of a teleseminar entitled "How to Use Craigslist as a Global Publicity Tool." To find it among all her other helpful tips and advice on getting free publicity, select "CDs/Transcripts" from the main menu of her home page.

means outsourcing work to lower-cost employees overseas, and typical pay raises are barely enough to keep up with rising gas prices.

The workforce has changed, too. Kids no longer graduate from college having a sense of what they will do for the next 5 years, much less the next 20. Thirty-year-olds are reading books on how to retire early. People who originally bought into the 9-to-5 working world are now looking for more flexibility in their jobs. Women who entered the workforce before having children have to decide if they will continue working, work part-time, work from home, or quit altogether after they give birth.

Do not wait until you have graduated, hate your job, or are pregnant to think about your North Star. That does not mean you have to put the vision into action today, but have a sense of what you want in your professional career no matter where you are at this moment.

When I graduated from college, I went to work for a wonderful financial company. I knew that eventually I wanted to start my own business, but I also recognized that I had much to learn, so I worked for the smartest people who would hire me. As you continue to work for a company in the short term or as part of a long-term plan, remember to always be acquiring new skills and thinking about the aspects of the job that you most enjoy. Even if you loathe what you are doing, chances are you find at least some aspects of it enjoyable. You might like the people, the casual dress code, the ability to work independently, or the group lunch you get to organize once a quarter. Pay attention to those little things because those are all attributes that make up the ultimate vision of how you want to spend your professional life.

Though you may be reading this book with the hope of making an immediate career change, the theory of using open innovation to become an everyday expert can be applied to the future as well. The Web may change and some of the technologies I write about here will eventually be outdated, but I believe we are only at the beginning of the vast and varied ways you will be able to create your own opportunities for fulfillment and financial success doing something you love.

Let the Money Follow

When you are passionate about something, you find ways to support your habit. You save money to buy new astronomy equipment or to take tennis lessons. You find time to attend classes or sneak away to your room so you can read. You sacrifice doing other things so you can indulge in your favored activities. Though you are probably reading this book so you can find a way to make money from your everyday expertise, you will continue pursuing your hobby or interest even if that never happens. And it might not. But my experience has shown that people who set out to do something they love can usually find a way to make money doing it if they have the confidence to try.

Of course, you can work in your garden from now until forever and never make a dime unless you start to employ the principles of open innovation and teach people what you know. Neighbors are not going to drop by and offer you money to tell them how to plant tulips. But you could become the tulip expert of the town or of the world if you wanted to. You could run tulip planting clinics, plant tulips for other people, enter your tulips in contests, invent a bulb-planting device that makes it easier to grow tulips, or you could start a web site to teach others everything you know about tulips.

If you pick an area you are passionate about and start doing it on even a small scale, your enthusiasm for the subject will draw others to you. And initially you will not care if you have one customer or a hundred, because you are doing something you love—something you would probably do for free. I give away my expertise all the time. I love seeing new products, and even if an inventor is not showing me his idea so that I can license and sell it, I will still give my honest opinion and feedback for free. I am passionate about what I do and am fortunate to have figured out a way to make money doing it.

Pursuing your everyday expertise does not mean you will be free from having to deal with problems or overcome challenges. But you do get to pick the kinds of problems you have to deal with. And that can make it a heck of a lot easier to get out of bed Monday morning.

OTHER EVERYDAY EXPERTS TALK ABOUT PASSION

Charles E. Kirk, founder and author of *The Kirk Report*[*]

My advice is that you have to find what you really love to do, first and foremost. Do not go into a business or a career only because of the money. Money does not bring happiness. To achieve a high level of success in anything, you must really be passionate about it and be drawn to the business or the career like a moth to light. That passion, coupled with hard work and tenacity, will enable you to live a great life as long as you spend your time doing what you really love to do. Life is too short for anything else.

Kelley Hill, Songwriter and Finalist in the Inaugural *American Idol* Songwriting Contest[†]

Rejection is hard, but in reality, it is just another challenge or obstacle to overcome. I had a song pitcher from Nashville pass on one of my songs. She said the song was good but she did not think she could make it stand out among the rest. I was disappointed, but I will not give up on that song. I believe it is a powerful song, so I will keep trying. All it takes is one person of influence to take it somewhere.

[*]You can read Charles E. Kirk's blog on the stock market at www.thekirkreport.com.

[†]Out of 25,000 entries, Kelley Hill's song entitled "One Night" was selected as a finalist in the first-ever American Idol songwriting contest. Check out Hill's other music on www.kelleyhill.com.

Lisa Lillien, Founder of Hungry Girl[*]

Turning a pastime into a business can be a big commitment, so you need to make sure you are really passionate about what you are doing. Part of the reason my business is so successful is because weight loss is an area that many people are also passionate about and need help with. I have had people tell me they want to create a business similar to mine only they want to discuss vintage cars instead of food. Then they want to know how much I charge for advertising on my site so they can do the same. That is an unfair comparison because the number of people interested in vintage cars cannot possibly be equal to the number of people interested in losing weight and eating better. You have to pursue the passions that you are interested in, but if you can touch people in some way with a personal brand, you will get more viewers and can ultimately make more money.

[*]Lisa Lillien's Hungry Girl web site is at www.hungry-girl.com.

FOUR

Uncovering Your Brand Potential: Personal Inventory

Everybody has the potential to be an everyday expert, including you. But while some people know exactly what it is they want to share with the world, a good many more have no idea and even doubt that they have anything worth sharing at all. But we all have life experiences, challenges we have overcome, hobbies we have pursued, skills we have mastered, and a million other pieces of information accumulated over the years that give us a unique perspective. With a little effort, you can use that insight to build a personal brand and go directly to the public, by-passing traditional gatekeepers like newspapers, magazines, and television, to share that expertise with others.

In the next section of this book, we talk about a variety of ways you can exploit your talents and interests to make money. You can start out in the beginning levels of open innovation simply by taking advantage of user-driven businesses and entering innovation contests. Or you can be a little more entrepreneurial and lay the groundwork for building a microbusiness that could eventually turn into a full-time business. But before you get started in either direction, you need to figure out which talents and interests to pursue.

A friend recently told me about a woman who, after years of dreaming of quitting her job to pursue more creative efforts, finally did it. She walked out the door of her employer's office and vowed never to return. Now, living off savings, she has 15 or more projects in the works. She has inventions she is trying to license, a book she is trying to publish, a song she is pitching to singers, and a work-at-home business she is trying to start. While I certainly applaud her enthusiasm and diversity, I worry a little about her financial future.

There is nothing wrong with having more than one passion, hobby, or interest. We are all multidimensional. But, as an everyday expert, you risk going nowhere if you are taking small steps in too many directions. Rather than do everything at the same time, pick a couple of interests to pursue and try them out. Better yet, look for a combination of interests that will make your insight, position, and brand even more unique.

PERSONAL BRANDING 101: WHAT IT IS AND WHY YOU NEED IT

Most people think of a brand as the name on the soda they drink or the emblem on the car they drive. While those are certainly important elements, a brand is much more than a symbol, a name, a logo, a consistent set of colors, or a summary statement about a product or service. A brand is a marketing tool companies use to establish a relationship and build trust with consumers.

Take the Nike brand, for example. If you buy anything from a tennis shoe to a golf club with that familiar swoosh on it, you expect to get a high-performing, high-quality product. You also expect to receive a Nike experience such as a boost in athletic performance, motivation ("Just Do It"), and respectability among other athletes ("She must be a serious runner because she wears the latest Shox.") Nike consistently delivers this message to consumers through its advertising, design, storefronts, web sites, and so forth.

Nike is an example of a traditional consumer product brand. A personal brand, however, has more to do with your unique point of view than with any particular product you are selling. Michael Jordan, for example, has personal brand equity because although he has long been associated with basketball, the Bulls, and a couple of other sports ventures, he has become an iconic symbol of hard work and superior performance. When Jordan puts his name on a product (any product), we believe it will have those qualities as well. Oprah Winfrey is a symbol of empowerment, integrity, and making a difference in the world. When she endorses a book or supports a cause, we believe it is worth reading or participating in as well.

Though you might not reach the celebrity status of a Jordan or an Oprah, your personal brand should be equally consistent and easy to understand. For example, you might be the "Green Gator," a person who promotes tailgate parties with environmentally friendly products. Or you might be a high school math tutor who specializes in helping kids raise their math scores on college admission tests. Whatever your expertise is, you want to continually reinforce the same message. The Green Gator should not show up with a charcoal barbeque, and the math tutor should stay focused on skills relevant to the tests she promises students will be able to master.

This is not to say that they cannot branch out at some point, but rather than go in an entirely different direction, they should add attributes that are consistent with the original platform created. The Green Gator could start to talk about environmentally friendly parties at home in addition to those held in parking lots and the math tutor could start helping kids improve their English scores as well as math scores on college application tests. Both extensions, though slightly off topic from the original business, are logical next steps and will keep consumers from getting confused or disenchanted with the new, expanded view.

If you already know exactly what your everyday expertise will be and are anxious to hear the ways in which you can use it, then jump to the next section of this book and get started. If you are not sure what your mark will be, however, find a pencil and some paper, turn off the tube, and get ready for a little self-analysis. We need to ferret out your expertise or boil down the many ideas swirling around in your head to figure out what combination will give you the best possible chances for success.

First, a word of caution. While this chapter is meant to help you derive the basis of a strategy for making money from what you already know, simply completing the exercises will not give you a crystal-clear plan for landing on the cover of *Entrepreneur* magazine. Rather, use the prompts to start thinking about areas you will explore as you continue learning about open innovation opportunities.

We also need to start with three ground rules.

1. *Put it all out there.* You are not allowed to edit or discount characteristics that you do not think are interesting, unique, or valuable. By itself, any one characteristic might not be any of those things. But a combination of characteristics might give you a huge distinction in the marketplace. Lauren Traub Teton, for example, created a microbusiness based on her age and her interest. At 40-something years old, Teton wanted to learn how to snowboard, but she did not want to get hurt. In looking for resources to help her learn, Teton discovered that all the information, products, shops, and services were geared toward male teens and college students who seemed more into style and speed than safety. Half of the stuff she did not even understand, and the kids on the slopes were more likely to raise an eyebrow than lend a hand. So Teton learned about snowboarding and wrote an article about snowboarding safely. She then created a web site called SnowboardSecrets.com to share what she had learned, to communicate with other snowboarders, and to post information on safe riding.[1] Her age and

---

[1]SnowboardSecrets.com is Lauren Traub Teton's snowboarding web site which can be found at www.snowboardsecrets.com.

interest combined gave her a unique voice in the world of snowboarding.

2. *Do not confuse being an everyday expert with having all the answers.* When Teton launched SnowboardSecrets.com, she did not have many secrets to share. But she added information as she learned and invited other snowboarders to contribute expertise as well. Though Teton is now an accomplished snowboarder with a web site full of everyday expertise, she did not start out that way.

3. *Do not worry about the "how."* We are working to uncover several areas in which you have insight, interest, and knowledge. For now, focus on what you know rather than how you will be able to use that knowledge. If you bog down on questions like, "How can I make money in an online world when my skill set is hands-on?" you are getting too far ahead of yourself.

It's All about You

In the pages ahead, I ask you to answer some questions about your hobbies, interests, day-to-day activities, work experience, education, quirks, unique knowledge, and even your genetics—all things that make you uniquely you. Along the way, I also cite some examples of people who used those seemingly small aspects of their life to make money—just to prove that these questions are important and worth taking your time answering, in order to realize your full potential.

Self-Assessment 1: What Gender Are You? (Gender)

We start with an easy question: Are you a man or a woman? That may seem too simple, but you may have noticed that there are a few differences between the sexes, and being from one camp usually gives you a different perspective from most of the people in the other camp. Just ask Lee Carlson, founder of the Dull Men's Club.[2] He created an online community so men with ordinary

---

[2]The Dull Men's Club, founded by Lee Carlson, can be found online at www.dullmen .com. If you visit the site, enter quietly and try not to cause a ruckus. We do not want to stir up any excitement for the guys.

experiences and modest goals could communicate with one another, free from the pressures to be trendy or impress others. Women are not allowed in the club because Carlson believes women are too exciting to be dull, would take offense at being called "dull," and might try to rearrange the furniture in the dull men's chat room. He is probably right. So, besides wanting the toilet seat to be up or down, think about your perspective on being a man or a woman.

- What kind of man or woman are you?
- In what ways are you similar to other women (or men) you know?
- In what ways are you different from other women (or men) you know?

Self-Assessment 2: What Is Your Physical Makeup? (Physical Traits)

I am not trying to be superficial here. The truth is, physical characteristics and genetic heritage can play a big role in the way we view life, make buying decisions, decide what activities to participate in, and so forth. For example, a guy over 6'8″ tall might have to buy his clothes from specialty shops, order tennis shoes online, and test-drive several cars before he can find one to comfortably drive. A petite woman might have the same problems buying clothes, cars, and shoes, but at the opposite end of the spectrum.

Height is just one of dozens of physical characteristics—including strength, agility, endurance, coordination, susceptibility to disease, physical aptitude for specific activities, and so on—that impact your life. Consider all the physical characteristics, both obvious and those known only to you, that have an impact on your life in some way.

- Describe your physical characteristics (especially those that make you unique).
- Describe your physical limitations (hereditary, medical, or otherwise).
- Describe your physical strengths and talents.

Self-Assessment 3: What Have You Learned? (Formal and Informal Education)

Being an everyday expert does not require special training or years of schooling, but do not discount that aspect of your life. Basic learning of any kind—everything from traditional training to learning a craft from a grandparent—will likely complement your desire to pursue more passionate interests in some way. Nick Lindauer, for example, received a college assignment that would later change his professional career.

In an e-commerce marketing class, students were required to develop the basis for an online business. For the project, Lindauer, a hot sauce fanatic, created a web site called Sweat 'N Spice to showcase his fiery collection of condiments and teach people that "hot sauce" refers to more than just Tabasco.[3] He received high marks in the class and, a couple of years after graduation, decided to revive the project and turn it into an A+ business. He added e-commerce to the site so visitors could buy everything from the milder Cajun Power Garlic Sauce (a mere 3 on Lindauer's heat scale) to Blair's Death Rain Nitro Seasoning (a 10+ that makes my eyes water just thinking about it). The Sweat 'N Spice online store draws about 5,000 visitors a day and, at this writing, Lindauer is considering opening a physical store location as well.

Lindauer's business and marketing education helped him turn an everyday knowledge of hot food into a blazing commercial enterprise. Whether you use extensive educational expertise for a new innovation (a former journalism major self-publishes a book on writing effective press releases) or apply just one aspect of formal learning like Lindauer did, education of any kind can be the genesis of your new career.

---

[3]You can purchase hot sauce and other fiery foods on Nick Lindauer's web site, www.sweatnspice.com. But if you happen to know a few things about hot sauce yourself and want to join a community of other hot sauce lovers, you should check out Lindauer's Hot Sauce Blog at www.hotsauceblog.com, where several contributors review sauces, share recipes, and enjoy heated debates over topics like ingredients, flavors, and bottle graphics. These two sites provide a great example of pairing a commerce site with a social, community-based blogging site. People who subscribe to and participate in the Hot Sauce Blog are likely to click over and buy products from the Sweat 'n Spice counterpart.

From the summer school classes you endured in fourth grade to the photography class you took at the community center as an adult, think of the things you have been taught. Pay particular attention to those areas you did well in, truly enjoyed, or seemed to master more quickly than others.

- What have other people taught you?
- What classes did you take in school, and what did you like most about each one?
- Finish this sentence: I could teach a class on . . .
- What *Jeopardy* categories do you nail with 90 percent accuracy?

Self-Assessment 4: Been to the School of Hard Knocks? (Life Lessons)

Some of the biggest lessons learned in life come outside of the classroom. Often these challenges (or even successes) trigger people to reach out and communicate with others going through similar experiences. Judy Seegmiller, for example, a two-time cancer survivor, found herself in a new role as caregiver when her husband, Craig, was diagnosed with Alzheimer's disease. As a form of self-therapy, she started keeping a journal to record her thoughts, notes on his progress, and insights on how she coped with taking care of a loved one suffering from a fatal disease. Though she had thought one day she might make copies for family and friends facing similar life trials, Judy Seegmiller actually ended up self-publishing her book in order to reach out to a wider audience.

Life with Big Al (Early Alzheimer's): A Caregiver's Diary by Judy Seegmiller (2000) is now available in online bookstores and is used as a textbook in one university's nursing program.[4] While she is not using open innovation for profit, Judy Seegmiller has achieved her goal of comforting others and through her efforts is also generating more awareness of Alzheimer's disease.

---

[4] Judy Seegmiller's book is available on Amazon at www.amazon.com.

Maybe you have had an experience—positive or negative—that others could learn from. That is not to say you handled the situation perfectly, have the only view that matters, or are no longer going through the experience. It certainly does not have to be health related either. Just think about those times you faced a situation and thought, "Where is the handbook on this?"

- Did you go through a time in your life when helpful resources could not be found?

- In looking back, do you now think you could help others facing a similar situation?

Self-Assessment 5: How Do You Pay the Bills? (Work Experience)

Just like your education, your work experience can be either the basis for or the complement to your new brand. One of my favorite examples of using work experiences as a basis for innovation is Angie and David Porter.[5] Angie Porter worked as a professional pet groomer for more than a decade and tried every tool on the market to reduce shedding—the number one complaint she heard from dog owners. When she could not find a grooming tool to effectively remove a dog's undercoat, she pulled the edge off her clipping shears and found that if she held the piece at just the right angle, the loose, dead fur came falling out in heaping piles. The effectiveness of her technique both astounded Angie and thrilled the pet's owner. So David went to work in the garage and added a makeshift handle to the clipper edge while Angie added "FURminator Shed-Less Treatment" to her list of services. In a very short time, the new service brought in profits that doubled the money made in the prior 12 years of business.

As the couple worked to develop better prototypes, patent the invention, and iron out the logistics of manufacturing the FURminator deShedding Tool, as it is now called, the Porters started a

---

[5]To see a demonstration of the FURminator deShedding Tools and read more about Angie and David Porter, check out their web site at www.furminator.com.

grassroots marketing campaign to convince other groomers to be authorized FURminator Shed-Less Treatment facilities. The strategy paid off for the groomers and for the Porters. Their invention drew rave reviews throughout the grooming industry. When they finally introduced a consumer version of their invention on QVC, it generated $30,000 worth of sales per minute, or about 36,000 tools sold in a single day.

You can see why I suggest reflecting on past work experience—everything from bagging groceries as a teenager to working for a major corporation as an executive—in defining your new role as an innovator. Inventors and entrepreneurs often discover, in hindsight, that a resume full of seemingly random jobs ended up being the exact collection of skills and experiences needed to piece together a powerful background for innovation. Think about all the jobs you have had in the past (both the paying kind and the volunteer ones), and think about ways you excelled in each position.

- List the jobs you have had, including your responsibilities and what you liked most about each job.
- What parts of the job came easy to you (whether you liked it or not)?
- List any significant contributions or achievements you made in these roles.
- What service, product, or process was lacking or would have made the business more successful?

Self-Assessment 6: What Do People Ask You for Help With? (Other Talents)

I played basketball in college and even made the ESPN *Highlights* one night. (Actually, Michael Jordan made the *Highlights*. I just happened to be the guy he dunked on.) I no longer play hoops on a daily basis, but I can still school kids from the three-point line and teach them the finer points of man-to-man defense. And speaking of sports, I am an avid Chicago Cubs fan and can tell anyone the quickest way to get to Wrigley Field and which concession stands to hit if they want to grab a grilled dog during the seventh-inning stretch and be back in their seat before the crowd sing-along is over. Maybe I do not make money now using these seemingly trivial bits of knowledge, but I probably could if I wanted to.

What about you? Think about those times someone asked you for advice, an opinion, or help—particularly on a non-work-related project or issue. Are you the friend people call for help installing crown molding? Or the weekend gardener neighbors watch to see when the rose bushes should be trimmed? Can you host a party for 50 guests and make it look easy? What other bits of knowledge and expertise have you collected over the years?

- What can you do with little effort that other people struggle to master?

- On what topics do people routinely turn to you for advice or knowledge?

Self-Assessment 7: What Magazines Arrive in Your Mailbox? (Hobbies and Associations)

My aunt is a member of the Cracker Jack Collector's Association (yes, there really is one).[6] In fact, not only is she a member, but she has one of the largest Cracker Jack prize collections in the world. Your hobbies and interests may not be as quirky but should still be explored. Do you scrapbook or collect stamps? Are you in search of the world's best Caesar salad? Are you good at magic tricks or teaching your dog stupid pet tricks? If you had all the time in the world and a money tree in your backyard, how would you spend your time?

- List your hobbies and interests.
- Describe a perfect day.
- If someone gave you $5 million, how would you spend your days? (*After* you got back from your vacation and moved into the new house, of course.)

---

[6]The Cracker Jack Collector's Association is online at www.tias.com/mags/cjca.

Self-Assessment 8: Who Sends You Greeting Cards at the Holidays? (Relationships)

Part of what defines you is the relationships you have with other people. Be they good or bad, those associations lead to expertise that others may not share. For example, only a stepparent knows firsthand how the dynamics of a home get shifted around each time the stepchildren come for a visit. But only a stepchild knows how it feels to be the one causing the shift. And only a parent sitting in the middle of both relationships knows how difficult it can be to keep even the happiest arrangements in harmony.

Within each relationship, you probably also have a unique role. Being a dad, for example, is hardly as simple as just listing dependents on an income tax form. There are about 30 million dads in the United States alone and probably close to as many distinguishing characteristics among those who are entitled to celebrate Father's Day. Combining some aspect of your relationship with another skill can add up to a profitably unique perspective.

Get out your address book, look at your e-mail contacts, and scroll through your phone directory. It is time to explore your relationships to see if you have a unique perspective in these roles.

- What are the (nice) names people call you?
- What differences distinguish you from others in these same relationships?
- What unique experiences have you shared with these people?

Self-Assessment 9: Oh, the Places You've Been! (Where and How You Live)

Where and how you live gives you unique perspectives and insight that might be worth sharing with others. Having traveled extensively before becoming a parent, Amie O'Shaughnessy suddenly realized she knew very little about traveling with a baby in tow. Her Ciao Bambino travel service was born out of a desire to figure it out and share her insight with others. Joe and Lisa Lynn host a podcast called Discover Woodfield in which they share their insight on what is happening in the Chicago suburbs.[7] Though the Internet makes it possible for both of these businesses to thrive in an area beyond their home towns, having knowledge about certain geographical locations is part of what makes them everyday experts.

Geography can also play a big role in helping you establish and leverage your expertise. A babysitter, for example, who is popular among the elementary school parents in her neighborhood, could start a Kids Club at her house one afternoon a week. Because the parents she sits for already know and trust her, she would have little difficulty filling the first class. She could then leverage the success of the first group and expand her business to other neighborhoods or age groups. Or she could take her expertise online and create a web site to teach other teens how to start Kids Clubs to earn extra money.

Whether you have traveled extensively or stayed in the same place all your life, the places you visit and the way you live your life could be of value to others. Consider that in answering the following questions:

- Where have you lived?
- Where have you traveled?
- Did you ever find something on your travels that you wish you could find at home, or vice versa?
- Have you figured out how to navigate something—geographically or metaphorically—that others might benefit from knowing as well?
- Do you have a local reputation you could parlay into a regional or national one?

Putting It All Together

Once you have finished your self-assessment, ask a friend to go through the list of questions on your behalf. This extra-credit assignment is sure to help you focus on your strengths rather than

---

[7]Ciao Bambino is online at www.ciaobambino.com, and the Discover Woodfield podcast can be found at www.discoverwoodfield.com.

limitations and will likely help you remember experiences you had not considered or even had forgotten altogether.

Then go back through the personal inventory and look for trends—interests that keep turning up, a skill set you frequently use, a knack for a certain type of work, or just hobbies and activities that you really enjoy. Also try to identify combinations that you could draw upon to establish a unique brand for yourself. If the answer is not obvious right now, wait for it. Think about the things you know, the skills you have, and the ways in which those two lists intersect. Let your subconscious brain work on the problem of determining your area of focus while you pursue your daily routine.

When inspiration comes, however, be ready to move on it because in the next chapter, making money doing what you love becomes a reality.

THREE EVERYDAY EXPERTS GET A MAKEOVER

PART I: PICKING A NICHE

In the pages ahead, we profile three people who are anxious to participate in the world of open innovation but still need to figure out how. Kelly Hales, a stay-at-home mom, would like to make some extra cash. She has a few thoughts on how she can make money, but her ideas are all old, closed-approach methods that are not feasible options while she has young kids at home. Steve Collins, my brother, is already following his passion of teaching and coaching. But he would like to make more money and reach a bigger audience without following the traditional career path for someone in his profession. And finally, Brooke Hall, a recent college graduate, has no delusions of job security in corporate America and would like to become an entrepreneur rather than an employee.

We start with the niches these three willing participants have chosen to specialize in. Later in the book, we check back in to see how they plan to take advantage of their everyday expertise using open innovation technologies.

Kelly Hales, Stay-at-Home Mom

Kelly Hales is a stay-at-home mother of four. She is drawn to the world of open innovation because she would like to supplement the family's income. However, she does not want to go through traditional methods of getting additional schooling or working outside the home in order to achieve that goal. In going through the self-assessment activities, Hales discovered she has at least four ways in which she is an everyday expert with a unique perspective in this world.

Hales likes to cook. Not only can she make a perfectly gooey Carmelita bar, but she has a knack for knowing how to manipulate recipes to bring out different properties—a chewier brownie, a flakier crust, and so forth. Like a musician who plays by ear, Hales does not need a set of instructions in order to cook a delicious meal. When she does use a recipe, it serves mainly as a starting point rather than a rigid set of instructions to follow. Hales finds satisfaction in serving delicious food to people.

Hales and three other women recently formed a dinner club. One night a week, each takes a turn cooking and delivering a homemade meal to all four families in the club shortly before dinnertime. Although the group has established some rules, such as no frozen or fast foods, for the most part each cook is allowed to make whatever she wants. Not surprisingly, Hales looks forward to her cooking day and spends most of the week planning what she will serve.

With four boys living at home, Hales gets plenty of opportunities to serve. From the food they eat to the clothes they will wear and the toys they play with, Hales has a pretty good idea what it takes to meet the needs of growing boys. This is not to say she has all the answers or believes herself to be a perfect

(Continued)

parent, but she does have a unique perspective in being the lone female in a pack of men.

A little-known fact about Hales is that she has twice won a great deal of money as a game show contestant. She won the Showcase Showdown on *The Price is Right* and, with her mom as her partner, won the Bonus Round on *Wheel of Fortune*. Though many people try out for these shows and never get selected, Hales has done well as a contestant because she knows how to play the games before she auditions and is not afraid to show her self-described "hyper" personality.

While Hales could find ways to be an everyday expert on raising boys, teaching people how to get on game shows, and so forth, she is very keen on cooking. And the dinner club is a unique way in which she uses her cooking skills. Knowing that many women struggle to put delicious and nutritious meals on the table every night, Hales would like to teach others how to organize dinner clubs of their own.

In addition to publicizing some of her favorite recipes and teaching people how to modify and expand recipes of their own, Hales looks forward to sharing her insight on how to pick the right group of women, establish ground rules, work out problems, and deliver meals cost-effectively. And the best part about being a dinner club expert is that Hales can do it all from home.

Steve Collins, High School Math Teacher and Basketball Coach

Steve Collins is a high school math teacher. But he is also one of the most successful high school boys' basketball coaches in Wisconsin. When Collins took over the program he currently coaches in 1998, the team had only once finished higher than fourth place in their conference in over 30 years, more often landing closer to sixth place or worse. But in the nine years since he became coach, the team dramatically improved, finishing in first or second place for the past six years and winning multiple conference, regional, and sectional titles as well as one state championship.

Under Collins' guidance, six players have received full scholarships to play basketball at Division I colleges after graduation, and, amazingly three of those players have also been named "Mr. Basketball," the highest honor a Wisconsin high school basketball player can receive.

The program has blossomed under Collins' direction because he strives to develop kids into well-rounded athletes who work hard, have sound basketball fundamentals, are academically engaged, and take pride in their school. He also works with everybody from the athletic department to the cheerleading squad, janitorial staff, and booster club to ensure all aspects of the program are of the highest quality.

My brother knows exactly what he is passionate about because he lives it every day. Why else would a guy spend eight hours a day in the gym for as little as $2,000 a year in extra pay? Though he would like to make more money doing what he loves, at this point in his life (married with two young kids) Collins has no desire to move into college or professional-level coaching. Instead, he would simply like to find a way to make more money doing what he already loves to do—groom talented young basketball players into high school stars and college-level prospects.

Brooke Hall, Recent Graduate

Brooke Hall worked part-time jobs while going to college and just graduated with a degree in digital graphics. Although one combination of interests has been swirling around her for the past couple of years, she did not even recognize it until we

(Continued)

started going through these questions. See if you, too, can spot what I saw.

Though she worked a few random jobs in high school, Hall's part-time work while going to college has been more strategic: learning the graphics business she ultimately wants to run. She worked for a Web development company for a few years and has also done freelance Web design for family and associates. In addition to Web graphics, she has designed everything from wedding and birthday invitations to programs and posters.

Hall then took a job working as a design assistant for a home makeover television show, which led to a couple of production-assistant jobs on other home makeover shows such as HGTV's *Design Remix* and *Color Splash*. When her school schedule got in the way of the production shoots, she had to find another opportunity. So she went to work as a marketing specialist for a real estate firm where she did everything from creating home sales flyers to uploading virtual tours and finding new ways to help Realtors market homes.

In her personal life, Hall and her husband have bought two homes. Though they fixed both up for sale, they sold one and ended up renting the other. A confirmed Craigslist junkie, she frequently buys furniture inexpensively and gives it new life. She is also a power user for a web site called MyPlace2Sell (think Craigslist meets YouTube).[*] Although the site offers people the chance to buy and sell almost anything, it started as a place for home sellers to upload virtual tours of their houses so people could preview a home before actually driving over to it. This is especially important for people relocating to areas that are not local to their current homes.

For the past five years, it seems everything Hall touches is related to home improvement, sales, rentals—and sometimes all

---

[*]MyPlace2Sell is online at www.myplace2sell.com.

three. Though professionally she has been focused on learning how to be a graphic artist and designer, as an area of interest, Hall has learned quick, inexpensive ways to make home improvements, stage and showcase a home for sale, and use emerging technologies as a way to increase market interest in a home. She is an expert on giving a house *virtual curb appeal.*

Although Collins knew immediately what he wanted to specialize in, Hales and Hall needed to go through the personal inventory to narrow their interests down to those they enjoyed and felt motivated enough to explore further. Hales could simply create a web site to discuss cooking but she has a greater opportunity for distinction by focusing on her innovative dinner club. And Hall has so many creative design interests that it will be interesting to watch her explore and experiment in the years ahead. The next time we check in with these everyday experts, we will find out how they plan to utilize their talents and interests.

PART TWO

PUTTING YOUR IDEAS INTO ACTION

FIVE

Beginning Level:
Test-Drive Your Expertise

T he easiest way to begin participating in the world of open innovation is to take advantage of company-sponsored opportunities. Although new ways to partner with innovating companies are always being created, one of the most popular ways to be paid for your insight and information is through innovation contests.

My company, for example, partnered with office supply giant Staples to launch a nationwide search for innovative office products. In this search, anybody over the age of 18 had the opportunity to submit ideas for new office supply merchandise in exchange for a potentially lucrative licensing deal. Patents and prototypes were not required. Though not everybody who entered the contest won, several people managed to license their ideas and get a significant amount of publicity just by making the effort to enter the competition. We have helped big companies like Unilever and Welch's get ideas from hundreds of people outside of their organizations, and we even helped a major apparel company discover the next innovation in bra closures (one of my favorite projects!).

Innovation contests are fun to enter, but the winnings only go to the few people with the best ideas. User-driven businesses, by contrast, are almost exclusively built upon outside contribution and therefore offer nearly everybody who participates the chance to make money. Talent is still required, of course, but the winnings are not limited to a select few. Some examples of user-driven businesses are Threadless,[1] Helium,[2] Greeting Card Universe,[3] OurStage,[4] and Can Stock Photo.[5]

I like company-sponsored open innovation opportunities for new everyday experts because the companies provide an almost risk-free way to venture into the open source environment without having to start a business or invest a lot of money. You can dabble, experiment, and stretch your abilities as often as you like. The investment is minimal, and the rewards vary depending on the circumstances, but the potential for discovering your true calling is great.

In this chapter, we discuss the benefits of participating in company-sponsored innovation, the investment required, and ways in which you can make the most of each opportunity. We also demonstrate the range of involvement, showing how some people contribute often and are making good money, while

---

[1]Threadless sponsors a perpetual T-shirt design competition on its web site, www.threadless.com. Anybody can submit a design, visitors pick the designs they like best, and the most popular designs get made into T-shirts that people can order from the Threadless web site. Designers with several wins get invited to design in the Threadless Select club.

[2]Helium (www.helium.com) offers anybody the chance to be a writer. Contributors can submit completed articles to Helium whenever they want on topics of their choice or those called for in contests or marketplace requests. For everyday experts, the best way to use this site is to submit articles based on your area of expertise and then make sure your user bio contains a link to your own web presence so people can click over and learn more about you. Though the people who make the most money from Helium are the ones who write about popular topics, think of this site as an opportunity to showcase your expertise rather than a solid moneymaking venture—unless, of course, you are a writer. Then you can write about the popular topics to achieve both the goal of getting visibility and making some money.

[3]Greeting Card Universe (www.greetingcarduniverse.com) is a print-on-demand greeting card service that allows anybody the opportunity to upload and sell their own greeting card designs. The site is very artist-friendly, so if you want to try your hand at designing greeting cards, check out the site and pop into the user forum for insight and information.

[4]OurStage (www.ourstage.com) is an online competition for independent musicians, singers, directors, videographers, and other talented artists. Not only can people enter and win a variety of competitions, but they can also upload their work and get visibility that is traditionally difficult to achieve in the entertainment industry.

[5]Can Stock Photo (www.canstockphoto.com) is a microstock photography web site. Anybody can upload pictures, though you are wise to spend time looking at the Top 10 lists of most downloads, most uploads, successful photographers, and so forth before just throwing old snapshots up on the site.

others simply dabble and are happy to get a couple hundred dollars in prizes each year.

Regardless of your level of participation, taking advantage of opportunities created by other businesses can be a fun and potentially lucrative way to make money using your interests, insights, and inventions.

Innovation Contests

Sweepstakes and contests have been around for years. But a new breed of competition called an *innovation contest* provides fresh opportunities for everyday experts to earn anything from a prize pack to several thousand dollars.

In a traditional sweepstakes, you put your name in a hat and win money or prizes if your name is drawn back out. Though you may have to collect game tokens, send in box tops, or satisfy some other type of entry requirement, winning is mostly a matter of luck. Traditional contests differ from sweepstakes in that some additional effort is required to enter the contest, such as sending in a picture, writing a limerick, or uploading a video of your dog doing a trick. Entries are typically judged according to some well-defined criteria and the best ones win.

Innovation contests are similar to regular contests, but the company sponsoring the competition agrees to do more than just give away prizes. They invite participants to shape the products or services they sell; generate content for their advertising, products, or other marketing material; or influence some other aspect of their business.

What Is in It for Them?

Traditional sweepstakes and contests provide marketing benefits such as increasing sales, stirring up consumer excitement for a product, and building brand loyalty—at least for the duration of the contest. (People buy more burgers during a McDonald's Monopoly promotion, for example.) Innovation contests provide many of those same benefits while also giving the company consumer insights, product suggestions, and creative solutions—all by accessing a large group of inexpensive freelance workers.

Give 'Em What They Want

One of the primary drivers for allowing outside input is to find out whether consumers are interested in a product or service before it is actually put on the market. In a closed innovation approach, someone within the company comes up with a new idea or the next generation of an existing product, such as lavender-scented bleach. The idea might be a pet project from someone in authority or the result of fixed research like a survey asking customers what smells they like best (as opposed to asking consumers how they like the smell of regular bleach and what, if any, scents they would prefer to sniff while doing the laundry).

After the appropriate layers of management mull over the idea and decide to pursue the product, the other gears in the company start to move. The R&D group converts the idea to an actual product. The operations group figures out how to manufacture the product at the lowest possible cost. The marketing team crafts a brand strategy, designs the packaging, and gives the product a clever name. Somewhere in the process, the company gets input from a focus group or a few individuals and they rework any area that needs improvement. (The smell is too strong or the lavender smells more like roses.) Finally, the new merchandise rolls off the production line and the sales team goes to work. Only after spending all this time and millions of dollars in development costs will the company actually find out whether consumers will buy the new, lavender-scented bleach. I call this process *push development.*

Compare that model of innovation to the *pull strategy* used by Kettle Foods, maker of all-natural snacks like potato chips, tortilla chips, and more. For several years now, Kettle Foods has run an annual innovation contest called the People's Choice Campaign, where potato chip consumers review suggested flavors and vote online for the ones they like best. People who want to try the chips before they choose can purchase a party-pack sampling of the various options from the Kettle Foods web site. At the end of the campaign, the chip with the highest number of votes is put into production.[6]

---

[6]To read more about Kettle Foods and find out when its next People's Choice Campaign will be, check out www.kettlefoods.com.

When it first launched the campaign, Kettle Foods hoped to get a fair amount of media coverage and fan voting. Surprisingly, however, it also received an amazing amount of online attention from bloggers and other web sites. Fans, who got swept up in the fun, bought sample packs, hosted tasting parties, rallied support for their favorite flavors, and urged others to go online and vote as well. So, unlike the bleach company that has no idea how its product will ultimately be received, Kettle Foods gets widespread consumer testing, in-home use, and a fan following for the selected flavor before it ever even hits the stores.

Thus far, some of the winning flavors (like Spicy Thai and Buffalo Bleu) have turned into the most successful in-store flavor launches in Kettle Foods history. Not only do the chips sell extremely well, but the People's Choice Campaign has become the main driver of new flavor development at Kettle Foods.

Find the Best

The second reason companies sponsor innovation contests is to find new opportunities to exploit—new inventions, talents, business ideas, and so forth. The object is to help the company increase sales, gain market share from competitors, bump up the number of products or services in an already successful line, or quickly identify new areas for growth.

The television series *American Idol*, for example, awards a recording contract to the contestant chosen as the best young singing talent in America.[7] Dial Corporation sponsors the Henkel Innovation Trophy competition to find new products, processes, and designs relating to laundry, home care, cosmetics, toiletries, and so forth that will be rolled into their product line.[8] At BIG, we ran an

---

[7]*American Idol* is one of the most popular open innovation contests in the United States. We typically think of it as just a reality television show, but it is actually an open source casting call in which anybody can try out for a recording contract—breaking all the traditional rules of having to know someone in the music industry or to spend years trying to get a talent scout to recognize you. Now, in less than a year you can get enough public recognition to draw the attention of a record label even if you do not win the *American Idol* contest. As proof, *Billboard* charts are covered with ex-*American Idol* contestants.

[8]To find out more about the Henkel Innovation Trophy, visit www.henkel.com.

innovation hunt that helped Merchant Media find a paper cutter that scrapbookers are drooling over.[9]

In addition to getting new products and services to sell, the publicity from the search often sends a message to employees, suppliers, Wall Street, and other important constituents that the company not only cares about innovation but is ready and able to capitalize on it.

Our Problem Is Solved

The third reason that companies create innovation contests is to solve a problem from a fresh perspective. In 2000, Rob McEwen, then president of a Toronto-based mining company called Goldcorp, sponsored an innovation contest because he wanted to find a high-producing vein of gold that he felt sure ran through the company's property. Frustrated at internal efforts to find the ore, McEwen wanted to approach the problem differently than had ever been done. So he posted all of Goldcorp's mining data on the Internet and offered a substantial cash prize to whoever could most accurately predict the best place to dig for gold. The winner did not actually have to find the gold in order to win the contest. McEwen wanted ideas just as much as he wanted the precious rock.

More than 1400 scientists, geologists, and engineers from all over the world took the data. After weeding out hundreds of unqualified submissions (like the people who threw darts on a map and sent in their guesses), McEwen and his team whittled the entries down to 25 that they believed were extraordinary. Some of the methods used to predict the gold's location were totally unconventional, such as using applied mathematics, computer graphics, and sophisticated modeling to analyze an area that many of the contestants had never even physically visited.

Not only did McEwen find gold through the contest, but he transformed some of the company's exploration methods as well. And of

---

[9]"As seen on TV!" Merchant Media (www.merchantmedia.com) is a direct response television and retail marketer.

the 25 semifinalists selected, 10 were subsequently hired at various times to do freelance work for the company.[10]

Creative Outsourcing

Let's face it: Companies also sponsor innovation contests because the public provides cheap labor! Consumer inputs such as thinking of a new product name, writing a slogan, or creating a commercial are all creative efforts that a company would normally have to pay a high-priced marketing and advertising firm to provide. Idea contests inexpensively generate results that have traditionally required funding internal research and development or a consultant. And since the contests make good stories, the public relations job is easier as well.

Sure, the company has to pay promotion and operations costs along with the prize money, but the sum total of those expenses is outweighed by the benefits of getting consumer-generated content. Though not every innovation contest turns out to be a winner for the company (the make-your-own Heinz Ketchup Commercial challenge turned a bit bloody—ketchup makes a great special effect), contests and open innovation are increasingly coming together. Through innovation contests, corporations can lessen the risk of introducing new products and services, find innovative ideas to use, have their problems solved by a virtual staff of talented freelancers, and outsource creative work to the public at a fraction of traditional costs.

In the future, I expect companies successfully using innovation contests to find additional ways to access and tap consumer wisdom.

What Is in It for You?

Innovation contests give everyday experts the opportunity to influence companies, to win cash and prizes, and to validate their

[10]After running Goldcorp for 19 years, Rob McEwen felt it was time for new management. Not surprisingly, however, he took a different approach to making the transition. Rather than simply retiring and leaving the board to find a new CEO, under his direction, Goldcorp bought another company and asked the purchased company's management to run the newly combined organization. McEwen is now with US Gold (www.usgold.com).

A WORD OF CAUTION ABOUT CONTESTS

Unfortunately, contests and online businesses often draw out the scam artists. Donna DeClemente of DDC Marketing Group, who has worked in the contest and promotional marketing industry for over 25 years, says you should question any business that does not have a set of rules and a recognizable sponsor. You should also avoid those opportunities that ask for too much personal information. Asking some questions to qualify you for participation, such as your age or the number of children in your household, is acceptable. Asking you to fill out pages of information or give out private data like your social security number is not.[*]

[*]Donna DeClemente of DDC Marketing Group writes a blog about promotional marketing services. She occasionally talks about open source contests as well. Her web address is www.ddcmarketing.com.

expertise (if my product idea is good enough for Bell Sports, then maybe I really could be an inventor). Weston Phillips and his buddy Dale Backus cashed in on all three of these benefits when they won the Doritos Crash the Super Bowl contest.[11]

As teenagers, Phillips and Backus spent hours shooting home-made videos and experimenting with software on a computer Phillips's supportive father bought to indulge his son's production interests. Though they occasionally made money filming a family wedding or a friend's graduation, the pair figured it would be a long time before they could make any real money using their self-taught videography expertise.

After working at other jobs for a time, Phillips and Backus decided to start a small production company with the modest goal of helping local auto dealers improve their historically bad television commercials. But a few months into the venture, the creative duo

[11]New Doritos contests are posted on www.snackstrongproductions.com.

realized that getting auto dealers to change their traditional ways of doing things would be harder then they thought. While lamenting the situation in front of his computer, Backus noticed an online banner advertisement for a contest inviting people to submit a 30-second Doritos commercial. The winners would receive cash and prizes and, more important, have their ad shown on TV during the Super Bowl.

With the deadline only four days away, Phillips and Backus decided to enter the contest for two reasons. First, they wanted a break from the frustration of trying to engage local business owners in more creative advertising. Second, they wanted to prove something to themselves. If their small company, called Five Point Productions, could quickly produce a good commercial, they would have renewed confidence in their ability to succeed in the production business, despite their lack of success with automotive dealers.

Although the duo did not feel they needed to win the Doritos competition for the personal experiment to be considered a success, they won it anyway and received prize money ($10,000 to each of the top five finalists), plus enormous satisfaction in seeing their "Live the Flavor" commercial featured on one of the most coveted advertising platforms in the world.

Now casually known as the "Dorito guys," Phillips and Backus have a new view of innovation. Prior to winning the competition, they believed that to succeed in the production business, they had to start at rock bottom and work their way up one client at a time. But having skipped a few steps with the innovation contest, the two realize they are already capable of doing inspired work at a higher level and now have the confidence to approach opportunities more boldly. Doritos scored big in the contest as well. The company won industry kudos for their daring innovation contest and achieved the goal of connecting their brand with a younger demographic.[12]

---

[12]The "Dorito guys" can be found hard at work running Five Point Productions. Check them out at www.5pointproductions.com.

Though not every competition won will have a life-altering impact, Sandra Grauschopf, the contest and sweepstakes guide for the online content provider About.com, says entering contests can be a fun, profitable pastime.[13] Having won several thousand dollars in cash and prizes herself, Grauschopf points out that contests requiring some degree of creative effort are easier to win because fewer people think they have the talent needed to enter the competition. But everyday expertise such as snapping a backyard photo, writing a poem while waiting for the commuter train, or describing the concept for a new product is often all that is required to win these contests.

While Grauschopf does not distinguish innovation contests from other skills-based contests, she does see an increase in companies using competitions to prompt consumers to interact with their brands. And even seasoned sweepers get caught up in the fun of casting votes for things like the next color of M&M, simply because they see a direct correlation between their input and the company's response. She says many people believe that companies generally do what they want to do and essentially tell consumers to cope with what they have been given or find their own alternative. With innovation contests, however, consumer opinion matters, and this feeling of importance stirs people to take action, vote, or contribute. Though nothing beats the adrenaline rush she gets when UPS arrives on her doorstep with a prize package, Grauschopf agrees that seeing the impact of her input can be satisfying.

From influencing companies for fun to winning competitions that inspire you to follow your dreams of making money doing something you love, innovation contests offer a variety of rewards for individuals wanting to participate in open innovation.

---

[13] About.com (www.about.com) is one of the leading content providers on the Internet. The site is organized by topics ranging anywhere from wedding planning to dental care. Each topic is hosted by a guide who is an expert in that particular field. Sandra Grauschopf is the contest guide for About.com (www.contests.about.com). Sometimes the experts are credentialed and other times they are just everyday experts like you and me. You can even apply to be a guide on the site. Check out www.beaguide.about.com to see some of the available topics.

INCREASE YOUR CHANCES OF WINNING
INNOVATION CONTESTS

When a contest is first announced, I can almost hear the buzz over the Internet. But by the time the entry deadline comes around, many potential winners drop out because they procrastinate in putting their submission together, lose confidence in their ideas, or figure too many other (more talented) people are going to win anyway (so why try?). Listen, if you are going to profit in the world of open innovation, you have to take the first steps. You might not win; in fact, you probably will not. But if you try—and try to learn from the experience—there is a much better chance you will eventually figure it out.

To get you started, here are a few tips for helping you make the most of the opportunity.

- *Follow the rules.* I run contests all the time and, without fail, we end up tossing entries from people who failed to follow simple instructions such as "Sign the entry form"! If a recipe contest says you must use raisins, do not bother submitting a dish that uses dates instead. And if you are entering an invention hunt for juvenile bath toys, please do not send a craft kit just to get our attention, no matter how cool it is. That rarely works.

- *Be original.* Sorry, the gel pen has already been invented, and using a Doritos bag as an automobile air bag has been done. Via the Internet, you should be able to do some basic research to see if your ideas are truly new and different.

- *Get to know the brand.* Tailor your submission around the needs of the company. The make-your-own commercial contest for Heinz ketchup ended up a mess because people used the ketchup for blood, toothpaste, and a few other odd (or X-rated) applications. Though that kind of entry might make for some yucks with your friends and can be uploaded on YouTube for a little notoriety, it is not the image Heinz is looking to attach to its brand, and it will not win you any cash.

- *Put your idea into practice.* Before crafting your entry, buy and use the brand you are working with. If you are submitting an invention to a contest, try to make a very basic prototype. There is always something to learn in taking your idea from theory to reality.

- *Make a professional pitch.* Ultimately, the idea matters more than the medium in which it is delivered, but a presentation that is professional, visual, and personal ("What this product can do for *you!*") will draw more immediate attention than one delivered flippantly on a piece of notebook paper.

- *Know your limits.* Although everybody is invited to compete on *American Idol*, should all of those people really be going to the audition? Unless you are truly in it for the fun, your efforts are better spent on opportunities where you stand a legitimate chance of winning.

- *Test your limits.* That is not to say you should ignore opportunities that stretch you creatively. If you are a great bicyclist, for example, your inclination might be to limit your competitive involvement to contests held on the road. But your cycling expertise might be just the insight needed to think of a new bicycle accessory for a major sporting goods company or to write articles on bicycle safety for Helium.

- *Partner up.* Do not be afraid to partner with others who share your enthusiasm for the subject matter or those with skills that are complementary to your own. Brainstorming often turns a good idea into an even better one.

- *Do not spend a lot of money.* Yes, there are contests that require you to enter fully developed or patented products. However, most of the people who enter and win those contests are already working on an invention that just happens to fit the criteria of the competition. If you are using contests to dabble in innovation and test your expertise, then minimize your investment as much as possible. The "Dorito guys," for example, spent less than $20 on their commercial, and most of that budget went toward buying bags of Doritos.

- *Keep trying.* How many clichés can I use here? You will miss 100 percent of the shots you do not take. Nothing ventured, nothing gained. If you do not think you will win, you probably will not. Bottom line: There is no guarantee you will win an innovation contest, ever. Even American Idol winner Jordin Sparks was rejected by the screeners the first time she tried out for the competition. But if you learn from the process, get feedback where possible, and continue to stretch your creativity in this way, you might win the next time. Sparks did.

User-Driven Businesses

Unlike contests where the chance to participate eventually expires and the number of people who can win is limited, user-driven businesses provide ongoing opportunities for people to contribute and to make money. The best of the breed are those businesses making it easier for talented people to break into industries that are traditionally off-limits to newcomers.

Ernestine Grindal, for example, wanted to use her collage-style artwork to make greeting cards. But she knew that major greeting card manufacturers prefer to use only in-house artists and that others can take up to six months just to respond to freelance submissions with a rejection letter. So Grindal started a home-based business selling greeting cards printed from her computer to local merchant. Then she found out about Greeting Card Universe (GCUniverse), a user-generated business opportunity created by BigDates Solutions.

At GCUniverse, freelance artists are invited to upload their art and images and build a GCUniverse storefront to showcase their work on real paper greeting cards. The company also provides Card

Widgets (rolling slideshows of cards in a particular category or store) that contributors can put on their blogs and web sites to direct traffic over to the cards they have for sale at GCUniverse. The site is absolutely free to participants. There are no setup fees or maintenance charges, and contributors can upload whatever cards they desire as long as the images meet quality standards and pass a very accommodating review process.

The upside to artists is that they get paid a generous commission on sales when their cards are purchased from GCUniverse. But the real boost to contributors is that GCUniverse cards are also marketed via BigDates Solutions reminder services like BigDates.com and Birthday-Reminders.com. Additionally, BigDates Solutions powers reminder services for leading online retailers such as Barnes & Noble, Lillian Vernon, and Overstock.com. Customers who sign up for any of the BigDates Solutions reminder services are sent timely e-mail reminders of important dates and holidays. Each reminder includes suggested paper greeting cards, free e-cards, and gifts, all tailored to the gift recipient's age and gender. The greeting cards suggested in these e-mail reminders come exclusively from the GCUniverse repository.[14]

Though Grindal could submit as many images as she wanted, she took a methodical approach to opening her GCUniverse storefront. She first uploaded about a dozen designs to see how customers would respond to her art. Then she used the activity report given to contributors to see how many times her store had been visited, which cards were clicked on, and which cards were purchased or sent as e-cards. Using that information, she added cards similar in style and content to those already proven to resonate with consumers.

Grindal says the money earned through GCUniverse is welcome, but the ability to test-market cards and get exposure to thousands of customers she would not have been able to reach on her own has

---

[14]BigDates Solutions (www.bigdates-solutions.com) is the brawn behind Greeting Card Universe (GCUniverse) at www.greetingcard.universe.com. BigDates is a third-party gift reminder service for several major retailers. Because BigDates only suggests cards from the GCUniverse repository, artists who contribute cards to this user-contributed business receive a tremendous amount of exposure. BigDates powers the reminder service for major retailers all over the country, so artists get national if not global exposure just for participating in this site.

been invaluable. Her success at GCUniverse has also increased her confidence as a greeting card artist. She now has a three-pronged approach to making money in the $8 billion greeting card industry. She continues to test and sell her cards via the user-generated community, is ramping up production of cards in her home-based business (cards that sell well online also prove to be top sellers in retail stores), and is submitting her best sellers to traditional greeting card manufacturers for licensing and even more exposure. Though she continues to work through traditional stores and retailers, the user-generated business gave her the springboard and confidence needed to take bigger steps in getting her cards to a bigger market.[15]

Corrie Kuipers, another successful GCUniverse artist, approached the opportunity from a different angle. After spending time analyzing the cards already available on the site, Kuipers dedicated a couple of months to developing artwork that specifically filled those areas where she believed cards were lacking. To find new ideas, she studied the card market, looked for trends and hot topics, and then worked diligently to create original cards in those areas. Kuipers uploaded over 800 cards to GCUniverse and sold over 600 cards within a few months of opening her GCUniverse store.[16]

Though Grindal and Kuipers approached the GCUniverse business in different ways, they both used it as an avenue to make money and gain exposure in an industry that is traditionally difficult to enter. Like competing in contests, participating in a user-generated business is another good way to enter the world of open innovation without starting your own business or giving it your full-time effort—though people who do treat the opportunity like a microbusiness are more likely to succeed. User-generated businesses are also a good testing ground for proving (or improving on) your expertise.

[15]Ernestine Grindal's Greeing Card Universe storefront is located at www .greetingcarduniverse.com/ernestinescards. If typing that address is too much work, type "Grindal" in the "Search Cards" field on the Greeting Card Universe home page and you will see why her cards are so popular.

[16]Corrie Kuiper's massive collection of whimsical cards can be found on her Greeting Card Universe storefront at www.greetingcarduniverse.com/corrieweb. You can also just do a search on "Kuipers."

How to Spot a Good User-Driven Business Opportunity

User-generated businesses like GCUniverse are becoming increasingly popular, though the name by which they are referred to varies. In the newspaper or business magazines, you will hear user-driven businesses referred to as *crowdsourcing, user innovation, mass customization, wiki, social media*, and *citizen media*, to name a few. While the terminology may be inconsistent, the key elements of these businesses are similar. But some user-generated opportunities are better for contributors than others.

No Barriers to Entry

User-generated businesses are typically open to everyone who wants to participate. While not everybody will have the skills necessary to prosper in the environment, the doors are open and the requirements for entry should be minimal.

Helium, for example, is an online community that invites anyone to be a writer and to share insight and expertise on a host of topics. Can Stock Photo is a microstock photography web site where anybody who wants to can upload images for sale. And Springspotters Network is a trend-spotting news service to which people can submit information about cool new businesses they come across.[17] In all three of these user-driven examples, participation is free, there are no minimum or maximum number of contributions you can make, and the only requirement for entry is that your contributions meet quality standards.

Contributors are Compensated

Wikipedia, Wikihow, and a myriad of other wiki Web sites are mass collaborations that allow multiple users to contribute information and to edit the contributions of others.[18] If you are browsing

---

[17]The Springspotter Network welcomes reports of new business ideas and trends. You can submit ideas or stay abreast of new business ventures by signing up for their newsletter on www.springspotters.com.

[18]According to Wikipedia (www.wikipedia.org), a wiki is "a kind of computer software that allows users to create, edit, and link web pages easily. Wikis are often used to create collaborative websites and to power community websites." Of course, if you do not like that definition, log on to Wikipedia and change it.

through Wikipedia, for example, and come across an article on mountain biking that you think is seriously incomplete or inaccurate, you simply edit the article. Though these sites are quite popular (boasting several thousand active contributors) and amazingly accurate (some teachers are frustrated that kids are able to get so much information with so little effort), contributions are primarily anonymous and altruistic.

Wikis are great examples of open innovation—but you will not make any money or gain any recognition contributing to them. By comparison, Squidoo is a recommendation network where people share their expert knowledge on a similar range of topics by authoring and grouping content into a Web page called a *lens*.[19] Arthur Russ, for example, makes a living working with computers but hosts a variety of lenses pertaining to his other passions such as genealogy, model railways, medieval gardening, and Victorian culture.[20] Though he only makes a few bucks each month, Russ gets a share of the ad revenue generated by hits to his lenses. Russ is fine with that because he mainly participates for the fun of it and to occasionally draw traffic over to his own web site. Squidoo lensmasters who host more popular topics get more hits, draw more traffic, and get bigger ad revenue payouts.

Payout Is Reasonable

Most user-generated businesses that compensate contributors have a payout schedule of some sort. For example, when you have earned over $20, you can request a check for payment. The minimum dollar amount should be commensurate with the amount of money you can make on the site. If a company only pays a dollar for your contribution, but you have to earn $175 before you can get any of the money, you might want to reconsider investing so much effort. The

[19]Squidoo is another content provider on the Internet. Unlike on About.com, where expert guides are hired to provide content, anyone can be a Squidoo contributor and create their own *lens*. Squidoo can be found at www.squidoo.com.

[20]Arthur Russ has several diverse Squidoo lenses including Nathanville Model Railway Village, The Herb Garden, Victorian Culture Headquarters, and so forth. If you enter "Arthur Russ" in the Squidoo search field, you can find a list of links to Russ's lenses. In Russ's bio, you can find a link to his personal web site, www.nathanville.co.uk.

imbalance might be a red flag that the business is looking to unfairly exploit contributors rather than create an opportunity in which everybody (contributors and the company) can prosper.

Room for Improvement

You might think that an open innovation community would be quite competitive. After all, user ideas are sometimes pitted against one another, and the more people involved, the harder it is to get your contributions noticed. But surprisingly, these environments are quite collaborative. Jump into a forum on a good user-generated web site and you will not only see the forum moderator as an active participant, but other contributors welcoming new people to the site, offering congratulations, making suggestions for ways to improve submissions, and so forth. On the Can Stock Photo user forum, for example, newbie and seasoned photographers talk about their rejected photos, ask for help with model releases and other legalities, and seek input on new equipment and software. And the people on staff are just as active. If the forum moderator is basically absent and there are posts from disgruntled contributors, you might want to research the site a little more before putting effort into it.

Cross-Promotion Is Facilitated

The bigger story makes for better exposure. Besides your mother and the local newspaper, not that many people will get excited about one writer, artist, or photographer making some money. By contrast, a large group of people succeeding in an innovative environment can garner a great deal of attention. And while some people are taking part in these user-contributed businesses solely to make a few bucks, others are leveraging the exposure to draw traffic to their blogs, web sites, or other businesses ventures.

Though this will become more important if you decide to move into the intermediate or advanced levels of innovation, a good user-driven business not only rewards contributors with money, but also gives them credit for their work. Kelly A. Mello has a degree in writing, communications, and rhetoric from the University of

Massachusetts, Dartmouth. Yet she credits Helium for helping her get a job in journalism.[21]

While working for a clothing retailer, Mello started contributing to Helium and a few other user-generated content providers as a creative outlet and a way to share her stories with others. Over a short period of time, she uploaded over two hundred articles. By contributing frequently to these sites, Mello practiced her writing skills and quickly built an online portfolio that included winning a writing contest and being the featured writer in one of the company newsletters (prompting a local newspaper to write a story on her). Though the money earned is not enough to pay the rent, Mello says the recognition for her work impressed prospective employers and directly contributed to landing her a new job as a journalist in the field she is passionate about.

INCREASE YOUR CHANCES OF PROFITING IN USER-DRIVEN BUSINESSES

Thanks to the open innovation movement, the doors of opportunity have been opened. But that does not mean you should trip across the threshold without first doing your homework. In addition to closely following the guidelines for submission, here are a few things you can do to increase your chances of making money in a user-contribution environment:

Think Like a Customer

To increase the chances of having your work stand out amidst others, learn about the people who buy the content (or pay for advertising) and work to align your efforts with their needs. Ben Martino, for example, succeeds in the world of stock photography because he figured out that graphic artists and designers are not looking for random snapshots. They are

---

[21]Kelly A. Mello has written over 250 articles for Helium.com. To read some of her work, go to www.helium.com and put "Kelly Mello" in the "Search Helium" field.

looking to save themselves the expense of a costly photo shoot. So Martino shoots versatile pictures that can be used in a variety of ways and will appeal to many different clients. He often photographs the same subject in a series of angles, distances, poses, and so forth. By predicting what designers will be looking for, Martino not only sells his photos but often sells essentially the same photo multiple times.[*]

Practice

As with innovation contests, you are not likely to profit from every submission you make to a user-generated business. But where the number of entries is limitless and you have time available, you might as well use the opportunity to practice your craft.

Take the example of Keith Carter, who wanted to join the contributor community at Threadless, an open innovation company that sponsors a weekly T-shirt design competition. Anybody can submit a design, voters pick the ones they like, and the most popular designs get made into T-shirts. The winning designer gets a couple thousand dollars in cash and prizes.

Carter's first submission to Threadless was dropped from the voting process because it scored so low. But he kept participating and, after about six more rejections, he finally won. Now with at least four winning T-shirts to his credit, Carter submits a bunch of ideas within a span of a few months and counts himself lucky when one of those gets a good response. He says the key to improving is not getting married to any one design, but continually testing the waters with a variety of creations.[†]

---

[*]To see some of Ben Martino's work, go to Can Stock Photo (www.canstockphoto .com) and select "Browse" from the main menu. Then select "Browse by Photographer" and search for "BennyM."

[†]To learn more about Keith Carter's work at Threadless, go to www .threadless.com/interviews/keithcarter or look for Carter in the "Designer Interviews" section off the Threadless home page (www.threadless.com). Keith also has a blog at www.kcarterart.blogspot.com.

Learn from Rejection

Though not every service has the capacity to give detailed rejections or suggestions for improvement, most user-driven businesses have an active community of members who willingly give feedback if asked. If your work gets rejected, try to find out why and then do something about it.

Through BIG, I meet with hundreds of people each year, all coming to show me their inventions and product ideas. Though I have years of experience in this area and have worked with leading retailers and some of the biggest product development groups in the country, I encounter many people who stop listening the minute I offer criticism rather than praise. I am not saying that you have to agree with me. Just hear me out. As much as my goal is to help people make money, I am equally motivated to stop people from wasting money.

So if a person making thousands of dollars each month in stock photography tells you that your photo composition needs improving, you probably should listen. If the voters on Threadless routinely bump your designs from the competition, you probably have some learning to do. And if I tell you that your product is too quirky to sell at Wal-Mart, then it probably is.

Do Not Be Shy

The whole point of being an everyday expert is recognizing that you have knowledge and expertise that is valuable to others. But unless you take the time to showcase your talent and upload your efforts, no one will ever know it. And the beauty of the open innovation world is that you can demonstrate your expertise in a less egotistical way than had to be done in the old, closed environment.

If you are a tattoo artist, for instance, you do not have to declare yourself "Tattoo King" to convince people you know a lot about skin and ink. You could instead write articles about tattoos on Helium, start a lens focused on tattoos through Squidoo, and maybe even upload pictures of your work to microstock photography web sites. Take advantage of the vast array and ever-evolving list of user-driven opportunities to showcase your talent.

Insight Opportunities

Innovation contests and user-driven businesses get pretty good exposure because they are fairly new concepts and are trying to attract as many contributors as possible. But there are other, less visible ways in which people are providing input to companies in exchange for money.

In addition to serving clients who want to share in the mushrooming success of innovation contests, BIG works with other businesses who want to be part of open innovation but are not sure about which areas to involve customers. Or they just want consistent input in a less theatrical way. For those clients, we run BIG Insight Clubs and ask consumers to provide input on everything from the garden tools they use to the kinds of meals they make for their kids. The best contributors are rewarded with cash and prizes, and you can win more than once.[22]

Julie Savage, a stay-at-home mom and former schoolteacher, was a member of the Problem-Solver Insight Club we ran for Merchant Media (makers of Smart Spin, Perfect Pancake, and other infomercial products). In her first weeks of participating, Savage answered questions about cleaning floors and the state of her toilets, and confessed to needing some type of guard to keep clothes from falling behind the washer and dryer. For her efforts, Savage earned a few hundred dollars and a prize pack, then signed up for other clubs to win even more.[23]

---

[22]We have several BIG Insight Clubs in operation at Big Idea Group and are always adding more. If you want to start contributing insight, go to www.bigideaclubs.net and register.

[23]Julie Savage is a BIG Insight Club member and she has also been a finalist in some of our BIG Hunts. She has a web site of her own called Ideas to Grow (www.ideastogrow.com).

You can also find other companies paying consumers to review products, take surveys, do some virtual mystery shopping, and so forth. A quick scan today of the "ETC" postings in the "jobs" column on Craigslist, for example, reveals several paid study programs, including an offer of $125 to talk about beverages, $75 to give insight on the way you use technology in your home, and $50 (plus two games) to be part of an ongoing focus group for a video-game company.[24]

INCREASE YOUR CHANCES OF BEING A GOOD INSIGHT PROVIDER

To provide good insight for a company, you mostly just need to tell the truth. But there are a few ways in which some insight contributors stand out from the rest. Here are ways you, too, can make the most of these opportunities.

- *Fit the profile.* When companies select participants to be part of a market study, focus group, or insight club, they work to create a small representation of the larger demographic the client is targeting. And more than age, race, or gender, they are looking for people who fit a certain lifestyle. For our Garden Weasel club, for example, we wanted insight from the people who got down in the dirt at least once a week, fertilized their gardens, and were willing to try new hand tools. Though you might be able to fudge your answers to get past the entry gate, you will not likely have the insight needed to get our attention or win prizes if you do not really fit the profile.

- *Give detailed input.* Think of this as your old high school English assignment. Answer a question as completely as

---

[24]Craigslist (www.craigslist.com) is like a massive classified ad. Not only can you use the service to find out about focus groups, but you can also use this medium to start sharing your everyday expertise. I talk more about that in later chapters, but just remember it is free advertising.

possible. If you are asked what meals you cook most often for your kids, do not just say "mac 'n cheese." Tell them why you pick mac 'n cheese, which version you buy most often, and in what cases you would consider purchasing other brands. Be thorough. Be specific.

- *Do not just wing it.* If you are asked to try a product, try it. If you are asked to watch a video before commenting, watch it. You would be better off telling the company you do not have time to complete an assignment than trying to pretend you did. Your answer will reflect the amount of effort you put into fulfilling the assignment.

Finding Beginning Level Opportunities

Contests are starting and stopping all the time, and new user-driven business make the headlines almost every week. So pointing you in the direction of a specific contest or business is a waste of paper. Instead, I will give you suggestions on where to look for yourself.

Open innovation opportunities are often publicized in innovation forums. Hilary Clinton, for instance, announced a contest to pick her campaign theme song on YouTube.[25] Disney Pixar announced the Ratatouille "So You Think You're Funny?" stand-up comedy contest on MySpace.[26] Design competitions are posted on everything from Craigslist and Digg to design forums and design-centric blogs all over the Internet.[27]

In addition to the opportunities publicized to the masses, several others are announced in specific user communities where

[25]Although many viewers access YouTube (www.youtube.com) for pure entertainment, others are using it as a way to broadcast their talents.

[26]MySpace (www.myspace.com) is another place that users can look for contests and other open source opportunities. If you enter "contest" in the MySpace search field, the results will show a variety of open and closed contests. Some are silly, but others are legit.

[27]Digg (www.digg.com) is another Web content provider. If you find articles, videos, or podcasts online that you like (or dig), you can submit them to Digg. Popular submissions get higher visibility, more clicks, viral marketing, and so forth.

sponsors know potential contributors will be lurking. Several years ago, Betty Parham started a Web site called Cooking Contest Central to publish upcoming culinary competitions. Initially, she posted just one or two contests a month. Now, years later, she is updating the site with eight to ten cooking contests per week, and many of those listings are coming directly from sponsors who want to be sure Parham's readers know about their contests. Cooking contest enthusiasts have little need to look beyond the virtual walls of this web site for opportunities, because if Parham does not know about the competition first, there is a good chance a reader in the user forum will tell everybody about it anyway.[28]

So one of the best ways for you to find opportunities suited to your expertise is to visit well-trafficked web sites for people who share your interests. Product competitions are regularly announced on the United Inventors Association web site and in Inventors Digest.[29] Business competitions are announced in business journals and magazines, most of which have an online component so you do not have to subscribe just to be in the loop. And Talent Speaks posts opportunities for all things artistic, including design, photography, songwriting, fine art, videography, and more.[30]

As corporations and user-driven businesses enter the world of open innovation, opportunities for everyday experts to profit from their experience are becoming more available. People who take advantage of these businesses can make money, gain recognition for their skills, and increase self-confidence in their abilities. They can profit in a big way (win Oprah's Search for the Next Big Idea) or in a small, consistent manner (writing articles for Helium). And

---

[28]The Cooking Contest Central Web site address is www.contestcooking.com. If you like to cook but are not sure that entering a contest is worth your time, check out the Hall of Fame big money winners on the site and think again.

[29]The United Inventors Association web site is located at www.uiausa.org. Once you register, you can get answers to questions, referrals to reputable services, and find an inventor group in your area. I highly recommend selecting a user group to attend. Not only will you find good resources, but you will enjoy the camaraderie of others trying to achieve similar goals. A good magazine for inventors is *Inventors Digest* at www.inventorsdigest.com.

[30]TalentSpeaks is a web site for designers and other creative people. It lists several design competitions. Check it out at www.talentspeaks.com.

they can participate as time permits without having to start a business.

But not everybody has an invention to pitch or a talent perfectly matched to a user-driven business. And not everybody wants to toss their idea in with the masses in hopes of winning a major contest or being selected. If you want to participate in open innovation on a more personal level, use the everyday expertise you want to share, and maintain greater control of your destiny, the intermediate level of participation in the world of open innovation encourages you to be a little more entrepreneurial. In the beginning level, you can just respond to the needs of others. In the intermediate and advanced levels, you need to know what your everyday expertise will be so you can start to manage your own personal brand.

SIX

Intermediate Level: Find Your Sweet Spot

In describing the beginning level of open innovation, we talked about ways to sell your ideas and insights to companies. Participating in those exercises is an easy way to test your expertise, stretch your creative limits, learn from other experts, and train yourself to reach beyond the obvious ideas in order to stand out from other participants. To make money and to get recognized in that mode, however, you need to align your interests with those of the company providing the opportunity—send in a soda commercial that will appeal to teens, tell us something we do not know about women's underwear, submit a clever T-shirt slogan with the word *nutmeg* in it, and so forth.

At the intermediate level, the focus shifts to you. *You* decide what talents to use and what interests to pursue. But this is not as simple as just circling a couple of items from your personal inventory list. You really need to think about what you know in relation to what is missing on the market in order to find a profitable platform. Do not worry that all the really cool niches are already taken. There is still plenty of room in the marketplace for the things you know. You just need to be specific about the expertise you have.

As demonstrated by the people in our case studies, the intermediate level requires you to be a specialist rather than a generalist. Kelly Hales is not just a mom who likes to cook. She is a recipe doctor and an everyday expert on neighborhood meal clubs. Steve Collins is not just another successful high school basketball coach. He picks out sixth and seventh grade athletes and has developed a program to increase their chances of playing basketball beyond high school. And Brooke Hall is not just another young graphic artist. She uses home makeover tricks and her graphic design skills to get homes ready for sale by being an everyday expert in virtual open houses.

You should expect to spend some time finding your sweet spot as well. Both Hales and Hall had a variety of broad interests they wanted to explore. But only after working through the personal inventory, talking to others, and evaluating their strengths were the two able to narrow their general interests in food and design, respectively, to dinner clubs and curb appeal. And even though Collins knew immediately that he wanted to focus on coaching, he still had to whittle his interest down to a specific niche (sixth and seventh grade basketball players in central Wisconsin).

Coming up with a unique platform can be a challenge. You may even experiment with a couple of different approaches before settling in on one that both fills a need in the market and gives you satisfaction. In fact, I can almost guarantee your strategy will change in some way as soon as you get started. You may find that your everyday expertise is too narrow and needs to be expanded in order to garner more interest. You may discover that the weekend hobby you wanted to convert to a day job is a little monotonous when it is no longer just a way to relax. Or you might find that you are attempting to do too many things all at once and need to limit your efforts in order to do one thing well rather than five things poorly.

Remember, the intermediate level is a time for learning and experimentation. Every move you make should be as economical as possible. All you want to do right now is create a small experiment or two, demonstrate your expertise, and then find out whether people are interested in your point of view. Start there, see how the market responds, and then build upon that foundation by taking your business idea to the advanced level of innovation if the reaction is positive. If the response is negative or just mediocre, refine or change your expertise and try again. Continue this cycle until one of your experiments works and you either get the rewards you are after or get a sense that the platform you have created could be expanded upon or leveraged to reach even higher goals.

Create an Online Presence

I saw a flyer the other day for a baseball pitching coach. The flyer said something about a guy who had pitched in high school, college, and the minor leagues. I did not have enough time to read the entire page so I grabbed one of the tear-off tabs from the bottom of the sheet that had his name and phone number on it. Out of curiosity, I thought I might check out this everyday expert later in the evening. But somewhere between the shopping center and my house, the one-inch scrap of paper disappeared—and so did my ability to contact him.

While I applaud this guy for starting small and inexpensively, having the courage to put flyers up in the neighborhood, and wanting to make money using his special skills and life experience, I am disappointed that he did not have a web site address listed on the advertisement so I could remember how to find him. And if I really did need a pitching coach, I definitely would have wanted to learn more about him before picking up the phone to make a call.

Although printing a few flyers is a great way to start small, in order to really take your everyday expertise from hobby status to potential business, you need to create an online presence so people can find you and find out about you. Web sites today are what business cards used to be. If you have a business of any kind, people expect you to also have a web site so they can do up-front research, saving everybody from wasting time if the services offered are not what is needed.

At this point, the biggest decision you have to make is what type of online presence to create. You do not have to build something elaborate or pay for a customized web site. Instead take advantage of the many services that are low-priced and easy to master.

Blogs

I am a fan of blogs because they are easy to set up, the most recent entries are always at the top of the screen, and you can start sharing your expertise without having to build an entire web site-right away.[1]

Izzy Dean became a consumer product expert using a blog. After working as a graphic artist for several years, she stepped off the corporate express train and onto the mommy track. But when her husband would come home at the end of the day, her pent-up need for adult communication got a little overwhelming. He suggested that Dean write a blog so she had someone else to "talk to." Taking his advice, she started a parenting blog and, though only a handful of people read it, she enjoyed the adult chitchat it provided her.

Then one day, ticked off that a beverage company had failed (in her opinion) to adequately disclose all of the ingredients in a supposed healthy drink, Dean took her tirade to the blog and wrote a scathing entry expressing her displeasure. A couple days later, however, she wrote a glowing recommendation for a different product she had tried and liked. As the topics on her parenting blog turned more and more to product reviews, Dean realized that she wanted to specialize in that area.

As a result, she created a second web log called Props and Pans, where she and a couple other bloggers test out products and services, then write about their experiences. While they started out writing reviews on products of their own choosing, companies now

---

[1]Technorati (www.technorati.com) is a web site that tracks blogs and other social media. If you are not familiar with blogs, visit Technorati and click around to see some examples. Go to the "Popular" tab as well and you should find a reference to ProBlogger, a blog about making money using blogs. You could also just go directly to www.ProBlogger.net.

send free products to the group in exchange for an impartial evalua-
tion and the publicity the site generates for products mentioned.

Though Dean and her friends would traditionally be unqualified
to act as consumer products experts, the Props and Pans web site is
quickly becoming a resource for other consumers because the opinions are unbiased and the comments are representative of a typical
use experience. Dean gushes over the Dyson Slim DC18 vacuum
cleaner because it gobbled up Cheerios without spitting any back
out. Emily Snipes says the Toastmaster Egg Head Egg Cooker is
"Not So Egg-cellent" because the setup is confusing, the cleanup
is a pain, and the alarm is loud enough to wake the neighbors.[2]

Blogs are wonderful tools for everyday experts because they allow
you to share information in a personal, user-friendly way. But the
nature of a blog, viewed as an online diary, requires you to update it
fairly consistently. A blog that has not had a new entry in weeks
implies the author has lost interest or the business is not worth the
effort. If you are not ready for a daily or weekly commitment, then
choose a standard web site instead. Though you will not add content
as often, there is plenty of room to tell people what you are all about.

AN ENDORSEMENT IS MORE VALUABLE THAN AN ADVERTISEMENT

Lisa Lillien had been trying unsuccessfully to lose weight for
years when she finally decided to change her eating habits in
order to keep the weight off for good. Her primary weight
loss secret is *swapping*—taking high-calorie ingredients out of
recipes and replacing them with guilt-free alternatives.

Committed to her new lifestyle, Lillien found herself continually turning over food packages at the grocery store to read
nutrition information and talking to complete strangers in the

---

[2]Izzy Dean's blog site called Props and Pans is located at www.propsandpans.com. One of
the reasons Dean has such a high search engine ranking is because she writes about products
that people are likely to be researching. If you search for the Dyson Slim on Google
(www.google.com), for example, Dean's review will probably show up within the first doz-
en entries. Emily Snipes is one of the other Props and Pans reviewers.

checkout line about the foods they were buying. But when she took a low-calorie product to a food lab to have it analyzed because she thought the manufacturers were misstating the product's calorie count, Lillien realized eating right and talking about her choices had become an obsession.

She also realized she could turn this passion into a business because despite the number of web sites and resources already operating in the multibillion-dollar dieting industry, Lillien believed none had managed to create a voice or a personal brand that consumers could identify with. She wanted to fill that void.

Thanks to her marketing experience and years of working in the print and online entertainment business, Lillien knew exactly how to position herself—she is the friend a woman trying to lose weight needs to have around. So she set out to deliver a daily e-mail newsletter in which she would share her insights as though she were talking to another girlfriend. She calls herself Hungry Girl.*

But Hungry Girl is not just a good marketing strategy. Lillien is absolutely passionate about what she does, so everything on her site and every bit of advice she gives is totally genuine. Not only has that authenticity made building Hungry Girl an enjoyable pastime, but it has also made the business quite profitable. While her e-mail newsletter is free, Hungry Girl revenues come almost entirely from custom advertising campaigns.

Because she wants subscribers to trust her and everything about the Hungry Girl site, Lillien will only accept advertisements from companies she trusts and food products she likes. Though that strategy may appear to reduce the amount of advertising dollars Lillien can earn, it actually has the opposite effect because getting a spot on the Hungry Girl site also means getting a Hungry Girl endorsement. With nearly half a million subscribers to date who trust Lillien's opinion, that endorsement is worth quite a bit of money.

*The Hungry Girl web site is www.hungry-girl.com.

Traditional Web Sites

Shannon Kaye is a talented artist and decorative painter, but she would rather refinish a computer than work on it. Although she is a great example of an everyday expert and has managed to profit from open innovation opportunities, she did it with nothing more than a simple web site that included contact information, a sampling of her work, and a personal story about her approach to painting.[3]

After years of making a living doing things she did not like—such as property management, sales, and office work—Kaye decided to pursue her artistic passions and paint for a living. The early years were lean, but her hard work and expert finishes led to a customer base of talented interior designers and affluent homeowners. Yet Kaye's success led to a new dilemma. Standing on a ladder, reaching out at awkward angles, and repeating intricate patterns for hours at a time became physically grueling. Kaye needed a way to get off the ladder and still profit from her expertise.

Knowing that home improvement shows on Home & Garden Television (HGTV) and the Do-It-Yourself (DIY) Network are often hosted by everyday craftsmen, Kaye (with a little prompting from friends and family) submitted a video audition to a local production company specializing in those types of shows. A few months later, Edelman Productions called to say they had reviewed her online portfolio, had just completed shooting season one of *Fresh Coat*, a makeover show using just paint, and needed a new host. Kaye landed the spot and filmed four more seasons of the show for DIY Network as the resident host, designer, and decorative painter. Shortly thereafter, she signed an endorsement deal for Shur-Line paint supplies.

Before the open innovation movement, Kaye might have had to keep the paintbrush in her hand to pursue her dream. Instead, she became a microcelebrity by following her passions, learning while

---

[3]Shannon Kaye's web address is www.shannonkaye.com. Though her site is now full of pictures, tips, and information, for years Kaye's online presence had little more than contact information and pictures on it.

NEED WRITING HELP?

While many companies actually hire professionals to write their blogs and other Web content, in this experimental phase of becoming an everyday expert, it will be cheaper for you to write everything yourself. If you are not sure about your writing skills or just want a refresher to build your confidence, take one of the writing classes at Writers Online Workshops.[*] They offer a variety of courses, the classes are interactive, and the instructors provide personal attention even though you will never meet face-to-face. Another alternative is to hire a college student or post an advertisement on Craigslist to find someone who can give you some assistance for less money than a professional copywriter.

[*]Classes are available at www.writersonlineworkshops.com.

doing, and making sure people could easily locate and view her work online.

Social Networking Sites

MySpace, YouTube, FaceBook and a variety of other social networking web sites provide users with the opportunity to create and customize their own home pages for free.[4] While many everyday experts use these sites as gateways to their traditional web sites and businesses, others use these virtual locations to test their expertise.

David Crawford, a middle school media specialist by trade and a songwriter by nature, wanted to record a song on his new webcam. So while his wife and kids were out of the house for a few minutes,

---

[4]Social sites are web sites that encourage and create ways for people to connect with one another. Although many people use these sites to virtually hang out with friends and meet new people, they can also be used as a starting point for putting your everyday expertise on the Web. Three such popular sites are MySpace (www.myspace.com), YouTube (www.youtube.com), and FaceBook (www.facebook.com).

he sat in front of the computer, played the guitar, and sang the humorous lyrics he had written for Pachelbel's *Canon*. Then he posted the video on YouTube for friends and family to enjoy. Although Crawford had no idea how many people would watch the video (if any), he hoped a few would like it enough to refer others—thinking 200 viewers would be real treat. But he reached that number in a couple of days and in less than six months had well over 700,000 viewers (the number is still climbing). Crawford has since added more songs to his collection, and the number of people tuning in to hear what he sings next has grown phenomenally despite Crawford having done nothing more than put a couple of songs on YouTube.[5]

The nice thing about social networking sites is that they are easy to set up and easy to update. They also provide simple tools to upload video and pictures, post and receive comments, and get traffic statistics (how many people have come to your site). The downside is that your web site will also contain advertisements and busy graphics that you have no control over. In some cases, visitors will also have to sign up for an account in order to see your complete site. Still, if you are really experimenting with an expertise and want to see if you can get even a single bite of interest before stepping out on your own, these services are a great way to go.

Vodcast and Podcast Sites

Though social networking sites make it easy for you to upload content, they do not always provide ways for people to download and listen to recorded messages or videos at their leisure. In other words, if you want to hear Crawford's next lyrical laugher, you must go back to YouTube and watch the video there.

If you want users to be able to download your music, videos, or seminars to their computer or MP3 player, then you should explore the world of podcasting and video podcasting (also called *vodcasting*). Joe and Lisa Lynn host a couple of podcasts. The first is called

---

[5]The easiest way to find Crawford's videos on YouTube is by entering his username (ddbbcc333) in the search field on www.youtube.com.

Cheap Date Show, in which the couple tour different cities and give tips for finding good food and good fun on a budget at each stop. The second is *Discover Woodfield*, a sponsored podcast where the couple talks about what is happening in the Chicago suburbs. The podcasts are hosted on their respective web sites, but can be downloaded via sites like iTunes and PodCast Pickle.[6]

As the technological environment advances, there are sure to be even more ways to establish an online home base for people to get a sense of who you are. Though I certainly hope you take the opportunity to do more with technology, at the very least create a home page that includes your contact information and a basic description of your everyday expertise so that when people see your flyer on the wall, they can go home and look up www.YourPitchingCoach.com instead of searching for some microscopic piece of paper that is lying on a sidewalk somewhere. (You can learn more about ways to get online in Chapter 12.)

Attract Visitors

Once you have figured out the best type of web site to create, you need to fill it with your personal tips, tricks, insights, and examples. This will let people get to know you and begin to view you as an everyday expert. But the effort will be wasted if nobody knows you exist. So the next step in your everyday expert experiment is to find ways to draw people to your site.

Give People Something for Nothing

One of the best ways to attract visitors to your Web site is to give something away for free. Though that could be a physical product, it does not have to be. Post free information: "10 Ways to Rid Your Garden of Mice," a recipe of the week, or a free white paper on environmental issues in your area. Offer free downloads or samples of your work such as a song, a recorded seminar, or a royalty-free

---

[6]PodCast Pickle (www.podcastpickle.com) is a good resource for learning, watching, and uploading podcasts of your own. You can listen to the *Cheap Dates* podcast on http://4thtimearound.net and the *Discover Woodfield* podcast on www.discoverwoodfield.com.

image they can use. Make worksheets and templates that go along with your subject matter available online. Give references freely.

Though you may worry that you are giving away all your secrets, what you are really doing is converting visitors to customers. You are also giving them a reason to come back for more and to refer other people to your site as well.

Charles E. Kirk, an independent stock market investor, writes a blog called The Kirk Report. In this blog, Kirk posts his thoughts, views, and analysis of the market in an effort to help other investors make better decisions. Though he has now been featured in *Barron's, Forbes, BusinessWeek*, and several other top financial publications, initial recognition as a financial guru came organically through word-of-mouth referrals and links to and from his blog.[7]

VIRAL MARKETING

Over and over again in this book, you will read stories about everyday experts who started out with less than a handful of people interested in their insight and expertise. But through little or nothing more than word-of-mouth advertising, their audience grew to thousands of people. Though the term for this, *viral marketing*, sounds clinical, it is really nothing more than a friend sending another friend an e-mail that says something like, "You *have* to read this!"

When Hungry Girl Lillien sent her first e-mail newsletter, it went out to about 200 people made up mostly of family and friends. Those recipients passed the e-mail on to their friends and a handful of new people signed up to receive the newsletter as well. (Lillien celebrated getting a dozen new subscribers in one day!) As the viral marketing continued, the subscriber list grew until ultimately Hungry Girl had a large enough

---

[7]Though much of the information on The Kirk Report is absolutely free, people who wish to make a small donation to help cover the cost of running the site are invited into a "members only" section that includes Kirk's trading notes, a snapshot of his portfolio, and question-and-answer opportunities. Check it out at www.thekirkreport.com.

audience to attract the attention of traditional media to boost her customer list even more.

When *People* magazine did a small story on Hungry Girl, Lillien got a couple thousand new subscribers. When *Good Housekeeping* did a bigger story, she got several thousand more. Though the publicity from magazines and other sources has been terrific, Lillien steadily increases the Hungry Girl subscriber list by several hundred each day simply by providing helpful information and consistently delivering it in the friendly voice her readers enjoy and feel compelled to share with others.

Socialize

One of the best ways to attract people to your blog or podcast is to pay tribute to theirs. While I do not prescribe spending all day reading comments or watching videos on YouTube, a few minutes of strategic viewing and posting can significantly boost your exposure.

For instance, if you have a scrapbooking site that you want to promote, be an active participant in other popular scrapbooking sites. Make comments, offer advice, and answer questions asked by others in the forum. Doing so will help those people get to know you and see that you are somewhat of an authority on the topic.

While some forums allow blatant advertising, most do not. Rather than posting your web site or contact information in your comments (which could draw a hand slap from the moderator), a subtle inclusion of that same data should be added to your personalized signature and profile. Users who want to know more about this person who seems to have all the answers will take the time to look and even click over to your online presence to figure out how you know so much.

Do not let the size of the forum intimidate you. Martha Stewart has a message board on her Web site where you can enter your comments about crafts (which could include scrapbooking), and when Oprah does a show about "scrap-addict moms," be sure to comment on her forum as well. (Here is a tip: Daytime talk show producers actually read the viewer message boards. If your comments are helpful and your input is consistently insightful, you could end up on the show.)[8]

Going one step further, link to other influential blogs and web sites. Not only are you likely to catch some cross traffic, but your search engine ranking is likely to increase as well.[9]

Track Visitors

Visits are good. Repeat visitors are even better because it means your expertise is resonating with those who have come to your site. But unless you find a way to capture the e-mail addresses of your visitors, you miss the opportunity to connect with them on a more regular basis. I am not talking about cookies, grabbing IP addresses, or other things that happen under the web covers. I am referring, instead, to offering an opt-in newsletter, tip of the day, or some other form of free insight and information that will provide an incentive for visitors to give you their contact information. Collecting those names and building a database of customers will prove to be a valuable resource as you move to the advanced level of open innovation because you will have an easy way to offer additional products and services to the people who already subscribe to your everyday expertise.[10]

---

[8]Make insightful comments that demonstrate your expertise without pushing your products or services. If I wanted to post a comment on Martha Stewart's "Fit to Eat" message board in hopes of drumming up new visitors to my personal training site, for example, I might say something like this: "Thanks for the tips on ways to cook oatmeal quickly. As a personal trainer, I always encourage my clients to eat a good breakfast. But most complain that cooking healthy food like oatmeal takes too long. I'll be sure to pass along your advice! I also wanted to suggest adding dried apricots to oatmeal cooked in the microwave. The microwave softens the fruit and it is a quick and easy way to add fruit to an already healthy meal."

[9]*Search engine optimization* is a term used to describe ways you can modify your web site to increase your ranking (and therefore increase the number of people who find your site) on search engines such as Google (www.google.com), Yahoo! (www.yahoo.com), and Ask.-com (www.ask.com). A good search engine ranking means your site pops up toward the top of the list when keywords relevant to your site are entered. For example, if you enter "Big Idea Group" into Google, my company is at the top of the list. If you enter "inventor services" instead, you will have to click through a couple of pages to find us.

[10]Although you can get fancy e-mail address databases and figure out high-tech ways of gathering customer data, in this level we want to keep it simple. Add a "Mail to" field to your web site or see if the service you are using has a way to do this for you. Then keep track of the users who subscribed or opted in by manually copying their addresses to an Excel spreadsheet or Word document. That will make it easier to cut and paste the names when you send out your first newsletter.

Participate in Citizen Media

At the beginning level of innovation, we talked about several user-generated businesses that allow people to upload content. Unless you are participating in a wiki where the input is anonymous and often tinkered with by others, you can also use these user-driven forums to lure visitors to your online presence.

For example, we previously talked about two contributors to Helium.com who used the writing site to showcase their journalistic talents.[11] But others have used it as a forum to demonstrate their knowledge and expertise rather than their writing skills. Say a race car driver writes articles about racing. In his Helium bio, he writes about his passion for racing and includes a link to his racing web site. Clicking over to his racing web site, you can buy products and services, become a sponsor, or subscribe to his blog. By contributing to relevant user-driven businesses, this participant is increasing his exposure by driving viewers over to his home track.

Do Not Ignore Traditional Media

Though open innovation is on the rise, traditional media is not dead by any means. So do not ignore the middlemen who can help you reach other segments of the population. Newspaper, magazine, and television reporters, for example, are always looking for fresh stories and reliable experts to quote. As an everyday expert, you have just as much insight to give as the guys with the fancy letters after their name.

In addition to gaining favor with Google to make it easier for these people to find you as their needs arise, go ahead and offer them your services directly. You can find e-mail addresses for section editors, producers, and so forth through the online counterpart to practically any publication or news outlet. Some even write blogs of their own, giving you an open

---

[11]On Helium (www.helium.com), you can write about any topic you like. While some people use this site to hone their writing skills and build an online journalism portfolio, others use it as a way to publish the information they know on a particular topic.

door for posting comments that will demonstrate your expertise to those who have the power to put your name in print or your face on camera.[12]

You can reach a wider audience with a little less work (and less tailored message, of course) using online press release web sites such as PR Newswire.[13] But before you hit the "send" button, check out Joan Stewart's web site, The Publicity Hound.[14] There she posts tips and tricks to help do-it-yourself publicists garner media attention without looking like a dog.

Go Off-Line

For many everyday experts, doing something they love means rolling out of bed and working in their pajamas, using a wireless laptop out by the pool, and never having to drive in commuter traffic again. Though in many cases the Internet has enabled dreamers to turn this fantasy into a reality, the Web does not have to be used exclusively to publicize your everyday expertise. In fact, you will do well to combine both online and off-line approaches.

For example, post a recorded seminar on YouTube to reach people remotely but appear at a local tradeshow to interact with people in person. Use LinkedIn and Facebook to network with people outside of your geographic area, but participate in chamber of

---

[12]Want to pitch your travel expertise to someone over at the Wall Street Journal? Start with the online version at www.wsj.com. Look around until you find an article related to things you know. Then select the story and scroll down to the end of it. You should find an e-mail address for the journalist who wrote the story. Take the opportunity to comment on the article you read (offering subtle praise is always a good idea) and see if you can be of service. A pitch might go something like this: "I really enjoyed your article on first-class travel among politicians. As the founder of Travel Insights, I regularly speak with people who spend their time in the air. We are currently running a poll on our web site to determine the number one gripe among business travelers. You may be interested to know that, so far, having to leave expensive shampoo bottles at the gate is more irritating than waiting in long lines or having to sit next to a smelly person for a long flight. If you are interested, I would be happy to share the final results with you."

[13]Submit your own press release on PR Newswire (www.prnewswire.com) or PRWeb (www.prweb.com).

[14]The Publicity Hound is online at www.publicityhound.com.

commerce events locally.[15] Use technology as much as possible, but do not underestimate the power of physically interacting with potential clients as well. Many things in life are still best accomplished face-to-face.

FIVE ADDITIONAL STRATEGIES FROM THE PUBLICITY HOUND

Publicity expert Joan Stewart has a web site full of advice for helping everyday experts increase their exposure and gain credibility. She also writes a blog and sends out a free newsletter every week. Stewart is passionate about helping people promote their expertise. Here are just five of the many ways she says people can quickly and economically become recognized experts:

1. Use web site statistics to track what keywords and phrases people are using to get to your site. Although I write predominately about free publicity, I about fell out of my chair when the statistics on my site showed that I get more hits from the phrase, "how to write a bio" than any other publicity-related keyword. Use the statistics to create more products and services geared toward the things people are looking for.

2. Use Google Alerts to find out what is happening in your niche. Every night, I get an e-mail listing of new Web hits on "writing press releases," because I have a

---

[15]LinkedIn (www.linkedin.com) is like a business version of MySpace but instead of building a list of friends, you build a network of business associates. When someone connects with you via LinkedIn, you can see all of their business connections and they can see all of yours. Then if you need an accountant, for example, you might check out your buddy Paul's accountant rather than trying to find one on your own.

Although Facebook (www.facebook.com) has a business feel similar to LinkedIn, it is more of social network. Instead of connecting with people, you get "friend requests." But unlike MySpace, where you just become online buddies, Facebook friends are grouped into relationships like people you went to college with, people you work with, and so forth.

Google Alert set for that topic.[*] Then I go through the list and look for publicity opportunities. I get very excited when I find a blogger writing about my area of expertise. This opens the door for me to go to the blog, read the com-ments, and post a few expert comments of my own. I recently posted a comment to a well-trafficked site. Not only did the blogger respond to my comments, but he invited me to come on his site as a guest blogger.

3. Write and post articles that content-hungry online editors, publishers, and bloggers can use for free. EzineArticles is probably one of the best free article directories around because it has a high page rank, will give you a byline for your article, and will allow you to link back to your web site.[†] Post several articles to this service and I promise you will be amazed at how often they appear elsewhere on the 'Net.

4. Speak at tradeshows, industry conferences, and other niche gatherings for free. I speak publicly all the time. But I always bring a door prize of some sort that I can raffle off while I am there. Then I tell the people in the audience that I will send them my free newsletter if they write the word "tips" on the back of their business card and drop it into the raffle bucket. That way, I leave the speaking engagement with a fistful of new opt-in contacts to whom I can not only send my newsletter but market my other services as well.

5. Take small steps. There are so many ways to get free publicity that trying to do them all at once can be overwhelming. I tell my clients to pick three options. Do those. See how it works. Then pick three more.

[*]A Google Alert sends you an e-mail whenever new information is published on the web that matches your alert criteria. To set a Google Alert, go to www.google.com and either sign up for a new account or log in to your existing one. Then go to "My Account" and select "Alerts" from the submenu. You will probably have to experiment with this feature a bit. Putting broad keywords in your alerts will inundate you with useless information. Overly narrow keywords will prevent you from getting anything.

[†]EzineArticles is located at www.ezinearticles.com.

Get Rewards

Although Izzy Dean gets a kick out of receiving free products to review on her Props and Pans web site, she gets a paycheck through advertising. As a member of Google AdSense, Dean displays random (but relevant) advertisements on her site and gets paid when viewers click on a link.[16] She also gets paid directly by other merchants and manufacturers who ask her to run specific ads.

Advertising is a popular way to make money online without actually selling a product or service. The more traffic you drive to your site, the more money you can make and the more valuable the white space around your comments become. Although Dean could probably do more with her site in terms of getting exposure or actively seeking companies to send products for review, she has her hands full as a work-at-home mom taking care of two kids and is, therefore, content to keep her business status quo. Props and Pans has a good following, a good search and Technorati position, positive viral marketing impact, and advertising dollars that provide Dean with a nice second income.

But not everybody starts an online presence or builds a web site foundation just to make part-time money. Some everyday experts are hoping to achieve big-time money. Others are looking to catapult to the top of a traditional career ladder without having to start at the bottom and work their way up one rung at a time.

Amie O'Shaughnessy, for example, created a web site called Ciao Bambino with the initial goal of offering high-end trip-planning services to families traveling to Italy.[17] Knowing how hard it is to travel with children, O'Shaughnessy's point of distinction is that she only recommends places that she or someone she trusts has visited and would heartily recommend for little travelers. Positive customer referrals and good press brought several people to the site,

---

[16]Many people use Google AdSense as a way to offset the costs of running their blogs or web sites. To sign up for this service, go to www.google.com/adsense. After you are approved, you put the advertisements that Google deems applicable to your site in the white space (unused areas) on your site. You get paid money if a user of your site clicks on one of the advertisements you have posted at the time.

[17]The Ciao Bambino web site is at www.ciaobambino.com.

but O'Shaughnessy noticed that while some visitors did want their travel plans handled from start to finish, a good many more simply wanted to get her advice, find out where to stay, and then go elsewhere to book accommodations without paying for the pricey service.

So O'Shaughnessy adapted to the needs of her customers by putting her coveted property list online and creating a self-serve feature allowing visitors to both search and book accommodations for free. Transparent to the customer, O'Shaughnessy gets a commission on the back end from the rental property. Though she still offers the original concierge service, Ciao Bambino makes more money with less effort by allowing customers to have the information they need and do the work themselves. When that model proved profitable, Ciao Bambino expanded again by adding France, England, and Spain to the list of available travel destinations. Although the business has expanded and the geographic locations serviced have increased, the original Ciao Bambino web site provided a foundation for O'Shaughnessy to venture further into open innovation one step at a time.

Will Leitch had a different goal. Throughout journalism school, Leitch's professors repeatedly told students that the only path to success as a writer would be through the painfully slow process of trying to break into traditional publications. Leitch could not accept that. So, after working one year in a fellowship position for a college magazine and another year for an online sports magazine, he moved to New York to become a "real writer." But after a few years of working odd temporary jobs and writing freelance for a financial publication just to pay the bills, Leitch started to wonder if he had been wrong about circumventing the system.

Frustrated at the lack of opportunities, Leitch and three other disappointed journalists decided to stop waiting for a chance to write the stories they wanted to tell. They created an outlet of their own in the form of an online magazine called the *Black Table*. For just over three years, the friends met weekly, took assignments or pitched ideas to each other, and donated thousands of writing hours to the site. (They experimented once with a paid advertisement, but hated it so much that they dropped it three days later and never cashed the check.) Though the foursome spent an inordinate amount of time working for free, each hoped the effort would give them much-needed exposure and eventually lead to paid writing gigs.

Ultimately it did. The group proved professors wrong when the *Black Table* disbanded because one person got a job at *Esquire*, another went to work for *New York* magazine, a third went to *Philadelphia* magazine, and Leitch landed a dream job as a paid, professional sports blogger. He is now the creator and editor of Deadspin, the most popular sports blog on the Web, boasting as

OFF-LINE EXPERTISE

In this level of innovation, the beginning stages of publicizing your everyday expertness, a web site might be nothing more than an electronic business card and brochure. Although I really want you to get to the point of using open innovation technologies so you can make money without having to interact with every single client in your community, I realize you may not be comfortable making that leap until you have proven yourself qualified to teach others in a one-on-one setting. There is nothing wrong with that. Just be sure to have the virtual environment somewhere in your horizon so you can be working toward ultimately sharing your knowledge and insight with others in a one-to-many setting. That is where the residual money lies.

If you open a cooking school, you can teach 10 students at a time for $45 each and make $450. When the class is over, the revenue is, too. If you establish an online cooking school, however, you could create an electronic cooking demonstration that costs $10 to download. When 45 people buy the video, you will make the same amount of money as you would have earned teaching a traditional cooking class. But the revenue potential does not end there, because the number of customers for your video could grow well beyond those initial 45

> people. If you take advantage of free publicity, social networks, and other ways to do viral marketing for your cooking video, you could be making thousands of dollars without needing to go back into the kitchen for some time.

many as seven million page visits per day (over 700,000 unique visitors per month).[18]

Leitch readily admits that his resume of random temporary jobs and a few sporadic writing credits looks like "total crap" and nothing that would make a player like Gawker Media want to hire him. But Gawker hired him anyway because, despite a sketchy resume, Leitch had proven his writing capabilities at the Black Table.

Do It for the Love

If you pursue open innovation simply for the money, you might get disappointed. Sure, you could pick some hot topic to be your brand simply to get a high online search ranking and attract plum ad dollars. But will you find the exercise any more satisfying than what you are already doing?

The opportunity created by open innovation is not only the chance to make money in a new way, but is the gift of being able to make money doing something you love. In the intermediate level of innovation, you do have to put ongoing time and effort into the project—not a lot of money, but certainly a good chunk of time. In talking to people excelling at this level of innovation, it is obvious they very much enjoy what they are doing. Leitch, in particular, worked for free for many years in order to get where he is now. And Kirk is still doling out complimentary advice and expertise just because he wants to.

Bear in mind, you do not have to pick a high-profile topic to make money. The global community is actually small. Though a few years ago it would have been difficult to find an audience of seven people to hear your opinions on any given day—much less

---

[18]You can see archives of the *Black Table* on www.blacktable.com. To see Leitch's current work, however, go to www.deadspin.com.

the 700,000-plus who read Deadspin—online media lets you reach clear across the planet to find others interested in your expertise.

The only way to reach those people, however, is by using technology such as a web site. Once you have it in place and start to get exposure, those with similar interests will turn to you for advice and defer to your judgment. New customers will come to your site every day, and repeat customers will start viral marketing campaigns purely from self-interest. Reporters will seek your opinion, use you for expert testimony, and write stories about you. Manufacturers, marketers, and advertisers who fit within your platform will seek your endorsement.

When this happens, you will know that your expertise and credibility have been established, and you are now in position to maintain the platform and enjoy your success, pursue that dream job, or leverage your community and offer additional products and services at the advanced level of open innovation.

THREE EVERYDAY EXPERTS GET A MAKEOVER

PART 2: BUILDING A PLATFORM

In Chapter 4, we spotlighted three everyday experts who figured out what niche to specialize in. Now they want to take their expertise and test out the intermediate level of innovation by creating an online presence, demonstrating their expertise, and figuring out ways to publicize their talents. Let us see what they have come up with.

Kelly Hales, Dinner Club Expert

Kelly Hales and three other moms in her neighborhood created a dinner club to help each other put nutritious, home-cooked meals on all their dinner tables four nights a week. On an assigned night, each woman makes enough food to feed all four families and delivers the food shortly before suppertime. Though the concept is simple, the group had to work out some early issues regarding delivery containers, how much food to make, accommodating vacation schedules, last-minute emergencies, and so forth. But the group has been operating for several months. The families are happy and well-fed. The moms are less stressed.

The success of this innovative group has drawn inquiries from several other moms interested in starting clubs of their own. As much as they want to join, however, newcomers express apprehension about recruiting others, being a good enough cook, having time to make their assigned meal, and so on. Hales finds herself explaining the process and fielding the same questions over and over again. She has decided to take her expertise online where she can share all that she knows about starting a dinner club in one place.

Her initial brainstorming session led her to create broad categories of helpful information such as organizing a group, menu planning, meal delivery, and timing issues. In addition to sharing her knowledge on those subjects, Hales would also like to incorporate a comment section or a forum in which other moms participating in similar clubs can offer their expertise as well.

Initially, Hales hopes to draw relevant but random advertising through online services. But she would ultimately like to entice manufacturers of some of the products routinely used— such as GladWare, KitchenAid, and McCormick seasonings— to pay for advertising directly. Though Hales feels fairly confident that she can generate enough interest in her expertise to eventually move to the advanced level of innovation, part of her experiment at this stage is finding a way to balance the amount of time needed to build a resource against the amount of time she has available. To hedge her chances, she plans to start small by uploading information as much as possible, but

(Continued)

only referring people to the site when they ask questions about her dinner club. She may even work with the other women in the club to make it a joint effort.

Steve Collins, All-Star Basketball Academy Director

Many high school coaches face the same financial dilemma that Steve Collins does. When you divide their pay by the number of hours spent coaching a team—much less developing a winning program—these individuals could make more money working for minimum wage. But they coach anyway because they love the game and being involved with kids.

A common way coaches try to correct this financial imbalance is to run training camps during the off-season to make extra cash. Though Collins has done that in the past, he wants to be more strategic. To start with, he is building a web site to introduce the Steve Collins All-Star Basketball Academy, an invitation-only summer camp program for middle-school basketball players. Unlike a typical sports camp where everyone is invited and instruction is one coach to many athletes, Collins will handpick kids who have great basketball potential, already love to play, and who dream of being named "Mr. Basketball" themselves one day. Because of Collins' winning record and local reputation for grooming players into prospects, he believes parents will pay a premium price to have their kids enrolled in a more prestigious program.

Although Collins has ideas for how to leverage the platform once it is established, he wants to run a single camp first and see where the needs of the parents and players lead him. Because he is so well known in the high school sports arena and particularly in his area, he only needs word-of-mouth advertising in order to get the right amount of exposure at the intermediate level of innovation.

Brooke Hall, Virtual Curb Adviser

As a home buyer, home seller, and person working in the real estate industry, Brooke Hall knows firsthand the anxiety homeowners feel when their house has been on the market for a few weeks without attracting any interest.

Until recently, most people who wanted to sell their home turned it over to a realtor, who planted a sign on the front lawn, put an ad in the newspaper, and listed the house on the multiple listing service (MLS). Beyond that, all the realtor could do to increase foot traffic would be to tie a few balloons to the mailbox and stage an open house.

But that has changed. Savvy homeowners are going it alone, using Web sites like Craigslist, MyPlace2Sell, eBay, and so forth, to increase online interest in their homes. As the world is becoming increasingly electronic, Hall is uniquely positioned as a web developer and home makeover expert to help people give their homes some virtual curb appeal.

Because she is well versed in the technologies, Hall plans to create a blogging web site where she will talk about her own experiences in buying, selling, and renting homes. She will include links to web sites where homeowners can click over and immediately list their homes for sale. She will also offer free articles on ways to stage, showcase, shoot a video, and write enticing listings to attract prospective buyers.

Hall initially plans to make money through ad revenue and one service: creating digital flyers that clients can print or distribute electronically. Clients can take advantage of her service from anywhere in the world because all Hall needs is the digital pictures, contact information, and home details. Using templates she will create herself, new flyers can be created within a couple of minutes.

(Continued)

To gain exposure for her expertise, Hall will put postings on Craigslist and MyPlace2Sell, participate in user forums on popular real estate web sites, and use word-of-mouth advertising among friends, family, and the realtors with whom she is already working. Hall has decisively moved up to the intermediate level of open source innovation.

SEVEN

Advanced Level: Kick It Up a Notch

When I started Big Idea Group, I simply planned to facilitate open innovation in the toy industry. I knew from experience that there were many talented toy inventors who were unsuccessfully trying to get the attention of big manufacturers in order to license their products. I also knew that while some toy manufacturers were reluctant to work with outsiders, others were willing but had no method for doing so. Since I had contacts in both the inventor community and the toy industry, I felt confident I could bring these groups together in a way that all parties would benefit—including me.

Through a little bit of trial and error I built the platform for Big Idea Group, including developing a web site, going out on the first of many Roadshows, advertising my services to the inventor community, and licensing a handful of toy products. With each successfully licensed toy, my reputation as an expert in toy innovation grew. I could have happily stayed in that niche for a while, but my customers' needs led me in other areas. Inventors with clever non-toy products enticed me to leverage the toy innovation platform and expand into consumer products in general. Companies I worked with asked if my inventor network could brainstorm ideas to fill particular needs. So I expanded the model again, adding Big Idea Group Hunts to the services offered. The company has grown in other ways since and is sure to expand again as we uncover more opportunities for evolutionary growth. But the original platform of facilitating open innovation between companies and everyday people has remained the same as when I first set up my door-desk from Home Depot and worked by myself in a windowless room.

If you work through the open innovation approach and one of your experiments starts to show promise, then you, too, will be primed to grow a full-time business organically, without the risks typically associated with quitting your job to start a business. At the intermediate level, you build a foundation like I did. You establish your brand, get exposure, earn credibility, and start to see the potential for rewards. That hard work culminates in a business model ripe for even bigger opportunities. Customers ask more of you, technologies present new ways to exploit your talents, and the business of doing what you love has the potential to become your full-time job. This is an exciting time because you have the ability to change your life, quit your other job, and be that person others look at and say, "Why didn't I think of that?"

However, before you go from part-time dabbler to full-time entrepreneur, you need to know when to take the expertise you incubated and refined to the next level, how to exploit the opportunity you created, and what aspects need to be reevaluated before moving forward.

When to Leverage Your Platform

In business, we all work to reach the tipping point in which all the effort spent building and developing a product or service, crafting a brand, and seeking publicity begins to pay off. The product works or the service resonates with those who test it out. Viral marketing turns to widespread exposure. Small orders turn to big sales, and potential customers are calling you rather than the reverse.

The time it takes to go from idea to tipping point varies depending on the level of innovation you start with, the nature of the platform you plan to exploit, and the uniqueness of the niche you are targeting. Though I cannot tell you how long it will take, I can give you a few clues that indicate when it is time to leverage your platform.

When You Win

If you had success at the beginning levels of innovation by winning or placing in contests, making decent money through user contribution sites, or doing well in other corporate-sponsored activities, then opportunities previously off-limits to you may now be open.

Five Point Productions, for example, struggled to survive until the founders entered and won the Doritos Super Bowl commercial contest. After kissing Doritos for catapulting their names from obscurity to credibility in the advertising arena, the guys went back to work in the studio chasing new business with relative ease. Potential clients, who had totally ignored their calls before the win, welcomed hearing from the "Dorito guys."[1] Similarly, Todd Basche, creator of the Wordlock, a combination lock that uses letters and words instead of numbers, had little success getting companies to consider his invention (or even accept outside innovation) until he won the Staples Invention Quest contest.[2] Since winning that contest, however, the prize money, royalties, and publicity facilitated both Basche and his wife Rahn Basche quitting their jobs to become CEO and President of Wordlock, Inc., respectively. They are now selling their products through major retail distribution.

You do not have to win a competition in order to leverage the experience of participating in it. Many contests and user-generated sites let the public decide who walks away with the prize, so the winning entry may or may not be the best one. And it really does not matter, anyway. Getting positive feedback or recognition of any kind is worth a little clout. Kelley Hill's entry in the *American Idol* songwriting competition did not win, but she managed to get into the top 20.[3] That placement gave her some credibility, a little publicity, and a spike in new fans.

---

[1]When Doritos announced other innovation contests after the success of the Super Bowl campaign, even they called the "Dorito guys" to generate interest. Five Point Productions is found online at www.5pointproductions.com.

[2]After the success of the first Staples Invention Quest, Staples ran three more quests, including one for kids and one for store associates. See if more contests are announced at www.staples.com/IQ.

[3]Kelley Hill is a contemporary Christian songwriter. Her first CD, entitled "The River," is available on CD Baby (www.cdbaby.com), an online record store that sells albums created by independent musicians. You can learn more about Hill on her web site, www.kelleyhill.com.

The competition does not have to be on television either in order to be worthwhile. Use each experience as an opportunity to test your expertise. When you pass the test, you can apply for jobs in traditional careers using your new credentials or quickly go through the intermediate steps to create more exposure for your success.

When You Have a Community

The intermediate level of innovation is all about building a community of people interested in the things you have to say, do, or teach. Oftentimes building the community requires giving some of your expertise away for free. If, despite your efforts, you cannot seem to make any real progress in building a community, then you revise, refine, or reject the idea and try again. If you do manage to get an audience, however, then you can start to charge money for additional products and services.

Angela Hoy, for example, first started WritersWeekly.com, an online community for freelance writers, simply as a hobby. But when she suddenly found herself a single parent raising three kids on her own, Hoy needed to make money fast. So she quickly cranked out an e-book called *How to Write, Publish, and Sell E-Books*, put it up for sale on her web site, and emailed an announcement to all of her WritersWeekly.com subscribers. She made $700 on the first day, and so many people in the community bought her book that Hoy became the best-selling author at BookLocker.-com, the print-on-demand (POD) publisher she had used.[4]

When Your Experiment Is Working

You are unlikely to create an initial business foundation that does not need some fine-tuning. When you have worked out the issues, however, expanding upon a profitable model is significantly easier and less risky than starting a big business from nothing. When I

---

[4]Hoy subsequently bought BookLocker.com to offer both advice and POD services to the people in her WritersWeekly community. To learn more about freelance writing visit www.writersweekly.com. To learn more about self-publishing go to www.booklocker.com.

widened my focus from toy innovator to consumer products innovator, I had already gone through the growing pains of developing the web site, branding the company, working out the legalities, overcoming early obstacles, and gaining credibility. Though I still had to establish relationships with nontoy-licensing companies and learn more about the consumer category, many of the risks of expanding my business to include new products were lessened by the fact that I already had a profitable infrastructure in place.

Kim and Scott Holstein also have a very successful, nationwide business. But they got there one step at a time. It all started when Kim Holstein had an idea to create sweet-and-salty pretzels. With no real food industry experience, the couple did some research, asked local chefs and bakers for advice, and then started peddling chocolate chip pretzels out of a freezer chest in their apartment. Local coffee shops and restaurants placed orders. When the pretzels became a local hit, the Holsteins went after bigger retailers such as Barnes and Noble, Borders, and Starbucks.

Although the Holsteins had a successful business, they did not have brand recognition. Customers buying a yummy pretzel at Borders, for example, had no idea it came from the couple's business. The Holsteins wanted to build upon the fact that consumers loved their pretzels by developing a recognizable brand for themselves. So they submitted an application to one of QVC's national product searches and got the chance to pitch their pretzels at the Mall of America, along with hundreds of other contestants. After a few minutes of tasting with the judges and a few weeks of sending follow-up product samples to the QVC food buyer, the Holsteins got an order, went on the air, and sold several thousand units of their newly branded, Kim & Scott's Gourmet Pretzels.[5]

Kim and Scott Holstein built a business model around selling uniquely flavored pretzels not typically available in other pretzel

---

[5]When the Holsteins got invited to meet with the QVC buyer at the Mall of America, they thought they were going to a private meeting. Instead, they found themselves in line with hundreds of other QVC hopefuls. They managed to impress the judges anyway. If you want to taste one of Kim & Scott's Gourmet Pretzels for yourself, you can buy them online at www.kimandscotts.com. To learn more about QVC Product Searches, go to www.qvcproductsearch.com.

shops. They figured out how to do that well, then simply expanded upon the business by getting larger orders and seeking bigger opportunities. Had they started with QVC, the venture might have been risky. But they had already proven that customers loved their product and that they could manufacture and deliver large-volume orders. So going on QVC took some guts but did not require taking a huge risk.

When Customers Ask for It

Since open innovation is founded on the principle of giving customers what they want instead of what you think they need, pay attention to how your community is (or is not) using your services, then see if there is an opportunity for improvement.

When we could not fill a client's needs with the inventions in the BIG portfolio, we started Idea Hunts to give companies exactly the types of products they wanted. When inventors questioned needing to travel to our cross-country Roadshows, we gave them telephone and mail-in submission options as well. When people called or e-mailed with fundamental inventing questions, we added basic inventing guidelines, resources, and insights to the web site. And we found that people responding to Idea Hunts were confused about how much work to do before sending a submission, so we put sample submissions on the web site as well.

Customer-driven expansion is probably the best reason for moving from the intermediate stage of innovation to the advanced levels. If customers want more—more services, locations, information— then find a way to give it to them before somebody else does.

How to Go to the Next Level

Without open innovation, making more money typically means doing more work. If you are a piano teacher, for example, you make more money by teaching more students. With open innovation, however, everyday experts find ways to make money without physically interacting with every single client they have. Here are some of those ways.

Sell Content

Offering free content, such as a newsletter, blog, podcast, and so forth, is one of the primary ways to increase the number of people in your community. Once you have those people, however, you can sell additional information. Joan Stewart provides a brilliant example of this tactic on her Web site, The Publicity Hound.[6] Though Stewart sends out a weekly newsletter and offers several complimentary articles full of tips and tricks for getting free publicity, she also sells an amazing amount of content including special reports, CDs, interview transcripts, booklets of tips, and e-books. Using technology, a good portion of Stewart's revenue comes from people with whom she will never personally interact.

Regardless of the nature of your expertise (informational, hands-on, and so forth), think about value-added content you could entice customers to buy. A martial arts expert, for example, who entered the world of open innovation by teaching a course at the local community center, could increase revenue by selling a homemade DVD that shows him demonstrating all of the steps learned in the class to help students practice. He could self-publish an e-book on the most effective self-defense moves or conduct videoseminars and teach 15-minute self-defense classes to corporations.[7]

Experiment with different forms of content to see which ones work best. Stewart's publicity tips can easily be read or listened to, but the martial arts expert probably needs to explore more visual

---

[6]The Publicity Hound web site (www.publicityhound.com) is full of tips and tricks for landing free publicity. As an everyday expert, you first need to build a web site so people can find you. Then you need to give visitors a reason to hand over their e-mail address when they do. Make sure you have that in place before following Stewart's advice, because there is almost nothing worse than landing a big story, getting thousands of new visitors to your site, and then missing the opportunity to include those visitors in your community on a permanent basis. The best people to whom to advertise your new products and services are the ones who already subscribe (literally and figuratively) to your expertness. You cannot do that if you do not know who they are.

[7]In the old days, holding a teleconference meant one person picked up the phone and dialed another person. Then, if the phone had multiline capabilities, he could conference in another person. Nowadays, everybody calls into a service with a single telephone number and passcode. Though many businesses use this function to connect employees at remote locations, it can also be used for remote presentations. You can hold a seminar over the telephone or over the Web, including videographics or PowerPoint presentations to go along with the audio service.

ways to communicate with his customers. You should also experiment with different topics to see what people are most interested in buying. And remember, this is an experiment, so do not go out and pay for a professional sound studio or hire an expensive graphic artist to make everything colorful and glossy. You can always get fancy later and upgrade those items that sell well. In fact, updating your content is not only good business practice but is another way to increase revenue again. (The revised *Martial Arts for Beginners* e-book is now available and includes full-color pictures and a bonus list of resources.)

Sell Products

While I am a proponent of licensing products and services to bigger companies who will do all the work and give you a royalty check for coming up with the idea, I also recognize that there are times when you might want to bypass middlemen in order to offer your wares directly to consumers.[8] Selling products can require a bigger investment of time and money than is necessary just to sell content, but open innovation technologies make it easier than ever to create and sell goods to consumers.

Starting with the easiest products first, if you have a fun logo or catchy tagline that people like, you could sell promotional products through print-on-demand (POD) services like CafePress and Zazzle.[9] All you have to do is upload your artwork, pick which products it should be printed on, and then set those items up for sale at the POD site. Zazzle even has a widget you can put on your own web site so customers can buy your Zazzle items directly from your web site. You only earn a percentage of the products sold, but there

[8]Licensing a product means you sell the rights to manufacture your invention in exchange for payment, typically a royalty, which is a small percentage of every unit sold. Licensing is a great way for idea people to focus on coming up with the great ideas and letting businesspeople handle the details of manufacturing, accounting, sales, and marketing.

[9]On CafePress (www.cafepress.com) and Zazzle (www.zazzle.com), you can sell T-shirts, posters, mugs, books, CDs, and many other products that are literally printed only when ordered. You do not have as much creative control as if you hired a graphic artist but the sites have simple software that allows you to easily create custom artwork on your own. Save the investment in customized company paraphernalia for when you know your business experiment is viable and ordering mass quantities of logo material makes sense.

are no setup fees and you do not have to store inventory, handle sales, or process orders.

Sometimes it makes sense to become a reseller in order to sell applicable products made by other manufacturers. The martial arts expert, for example, could sell training aids, sparring gear, and other accessories he believes are of value. He could sell them online through his web site or just bring along appropriate products whenever he teaches a class (jump ropes to the fitness class and throwing stars to the weapons class). Although it may be enticing to start an online store and sell everything you can think of, selling only those products you personally endorse will make your site more valuable to your community.

You might also sell products you create or invent. When Laura Heuer's son fell ill she took him to the doctor, thinking it would be a simple trip. But a misdiagnosis and an allergic reaction to the medication he had been prescribed put her son in jeopardy and Heuer in a panic. In the midst of trying to figure out what her son needed, Heuer had been expected to remember events leading up to the illness, what her son had eaten, symptoms he might have had, family histories, and so forth. Having gone through similar family emergencies regarding her mother's health, Heuer decided the time had come to get the family's health information organized so she could take control of their medical care once and for all. Thus began her quest to create a complete health care organizer.

Although she wanted the organizer to be electronic, funds were limited. So Heuer focused solely on developing and manufacturing a paper-based version that included family history, immunization charts, prescriptions taken, a business card holder to keep track of the doctors seen, note cards for writing down questions and answers for the doctor, and so on. After the Jakoter web site launched and the Jakoter Health Care Organizer became available for sale,[10] Heuer came across an electronic organizer called MedicTag. Although MedicTag did not have all of the features Heuer wanted, she still

[10]Laura Heuer's Jakoter Health Care Organizer is available at www.jakoter.com and as a private-label organizer for Franklin Covey (www.franklincovey.com).

believed it could be a helpful alternative for her customers, so she started selling that product from her web site as well.

As the Jakoter business grew, Heuer eventually had the resources needed to expand her product line. First she created a purse-size version of the paper-based organizer. Then she partnered with MedicTag to manufacture the Jakoter Health Tag, an electronic version of the Jakoter Health Care Organizer. With each new product added to the Jakoter Health Care line, Heuer increases her revenue opportunities. She also lessens the time to market because the foundation (branding, logos, customer base, and so on) upon which the new products will be built has already been developed.

Although selling products also means dealing with potential inventory, sales, and order fulfillment headaches, it can bring a great deal of money to a business. Another benefit to selling products you create is that you can test-market products and use positive consumer reaction and sales data to attract big retail sales orders or potential licensing deals from companies who might have otherwise ignored you. Several BookLocker authors, for example, self-published books after their manuscripts were rejected by publishing houses, then landed traditional book deals when their books became popular.

SAMPLE PRESS RELEASE
FOR AN EVERYDAY EXPERT

Rather than sending out press releases to make announcements that nobody really cares about, give helpful tips and advice to position yourself as an expert. You can still promote and sell your products, services, or web site, but make that information part of a bigger story.

Laura Heuer is an everyday expert who took a family crisis, learned from the experience, and then turned her new expertise into a profitable business. She used the following press release to get national media coverage and establish herself as an expert on the subject of family health care.

For Immediate Release
Six Ways to Get Better Healthcare

Laura Heuer, of Jakoter Health Organizers, says tracking your family's medical history can empower you to influence earlier problem detection, a more accurate diagnosis, and better treatment.

Hawthorn Woods, IL, December 11, 2006—When Laura Heuer's son contracted viral meningitis and had severe allergic reactions to various treatments, she initially fell into an abyss of tests, prescriptions, doctor appointments, and conflicting medical advice. Then this enterprising mother of three decided to get organized and take control of the situation. Being organized empowered Heuer to help her son get an accurate diagnosis and it eventually led her to work with Franklin-Covey® to create the FranklinCovey® Healthcare Organizer to empower others to do the same.

Whether suffering from an illness yourself or providing care to a loved one, Heuer says getting organized and involved in the medical process can help you receive better health care including earlier problem detection, a more accurate diagnosis, and more effective treatment. Although medical terminology and procedures can be overwhelming, following Heuer's steps for getting organized can give you confidence and make the task less daunting:

1. *Start tracking your family's health history before there is a problem.* By keeping a running log of all health-related incidents (i.e., tetanus shots, flu shots, ear infections, prescriptions taken, etc.) for each member of the family, you'll be able to provide doctors with a complete and accurate family medical history if needed.

2. *Check out the family tree.* Compile a list of diseases and medical conditions that are common among relatives in your family. Identifying illnesses you are at a higher risk of contracting may spur the doctor to recommend preventative treatment or tests for early detection.

3. *Record symptoms and health-related activities in a calendar.* Having a timeline of symptoms can help doctors identify trends that may impact diagnosis. For example, flulike symptoms that occur at the same time every year may be an allergy rather than a cold. Migraines clustered around a menstrual cycle may be related to hormonal fluctuations. And more than four ear infections in a year could lead to more aggressive treatment than another round of antibiotics.

4. *Journal symptoms as they occur.* Don't wait until the doctor's appointment to try and remember every pain or abnormal feeling you've experienced since the last visit. Seemingly unrelated symptoms may prompt the doctor to try different tests or treatments than originally planned. Frequent urination, for example, may indicate a bladder infection. But excessive urination coupled with fatigue and persistent thirst may be a sign of diabetes or another more serious condition.

5. *Write questions and answers down.* Again, don't rely on memory to make the most of doctor visits. Write questions down ahead of time and then write the doctor's response next to each question. The personal Q&A will be a handy reference later and can assist in communicating with family members or caregivers who might have similar concerns.

6. *Keep everything in one place.* Keep all health-related documents, including family medical history, symptom journals, test results, immunization charts, list of prescriptions taken, insurance coverage, blood work, question/answer sheets, and so on, in one organized

binder. Having the information at your fingertips can be a real time saver and it can also help ensure everybody involved in taking care of an ailing family member has the information to do so properly.

With the FranklinCovey® Healthcare Organizer, getting your health organized is even easier. The Healthcare Organizer features a durable three-ring poly binder; forms and tabs for tracking Health History, Bills and Receipts, Appointments, Notes, Symptoms, Charts, Medication, Test Results, Doctor's Letters, and Resources; three blank tabs; and a sticker sheet with preprinted and blank tab labels. Plastic accessories also included are: two business card holders, one zipper pouch, and six sheet protectors. This organizer is available in the FranklinCovey® monarch size for $39.95 and is available at www.franklincovey.com and at FranklinCovey's 89 stores nationwide.

About Laura Heuer

Laura Heuer is the owner and founder of Jakoter Health Organizers, a company dedicated to offering personal health organization to families, individuals, and caregivers. Heuer partnered with FranklinCovey® to create the Healthcare Organizer because she believes highly effective people should also be active participants in organizing and managing their own health. Heuer likes to hike as much as possible with her husband of 23 years and her three active boys. Although her professional goal is to empower people through organizing their health, her personal goal is to raise her boys into three good men.

Sell Services

Selling content enables you to reach people all over the world without actually talking to them on an individual basis. But some people prefer the latter and are willing to pay for it. In addition to the content sold on the Publicity Hound web site, Joan Stewart also offers workshops, keynote addresses, and other consulting services. I also customize services at Big Idea Group. Though we have programs we believe will work for most clients, I will tailor a program to the specific needs of any one client—for a price.

Expand

Another way to reach more people and make more money is to expand your platform into broader categories, geographic locations, or additional sales channels. I first expanded my business into other areas of interest—for example, moving from a toy industry focus to consumer products in general. Ciao Bambino, the company we talked about in Chapter 6, expanded geographically. When Amie O'Shaughnessy figured out how to convert visitors to customers in an efficient and profitable way, she went from serving families traveling to Italy to servicing other European destinations as well.[11] Kim and Scott Holstein had a good nationwide business selling nonbranded pretzels before launching their name-brand gourmet pretzels on home shopping networks and in their own retail store.

Another way to grow is to replicate your model instead of expanding it. Gawker Media created a successful blogging-for-ad-dollars web site called Gizmodo, where a team of bloggers write about various gadgets on the market. They then launched a similar-format web site called Gawker to cover Manhattan media news and gossip. From there, the clones kept coming. Defamer (Los Angeles gossip), Wonkette (D.C. gossip), Deadspin (sporting news), Jalopnik (car stuff), and Idolator (music industry) are just a few of the many blog sites the company owns, all in the same format, following the same business model.[12]

When you, too, have figured out a winning platform, you can expand into areas that make the most sense or turn your model into a template and create a cookie-cutter recipe for attracting new sets of customers.

---

[11]O'Shaughnessy's web site is www.ciaobambino.com.

[12]You can see the entire line of Gawker blogs at www.gawker.com. Scroll down on the left-hand side to see links to Gizmodo, Defamer, and the others.

Checkpoint

We keep talking about proven platforms and working models. But what should you do if readership does not increase, nobody cares about your expertise, and not one person calls into your tele-seminar? Before you abandon the model, evaluate your niche from the following perspectives.

Demographic

I really think it is possible to find a community of people interested in almost anything. Though I suppose your niche might be too small, it is more likely that you have not found a way to reach them. Or perhaps the people in your targeted community are not technically savvy enough to reach using virtual methods. If this is the case, you need to either reevaluate your position or get more creative.

The best way to reach nontechnical people is to use traditional media. You will have to work more aggressively to put out good press releases and media pitches that promote your expertise in order to get featured in newspapers, magazines, and other old-school communication methods. Of course, you need to put that effort toward publications your audience is likely to read. Getting on the cover of *Wired* magazine will make a cool picture for your office, but it is unlikely to increase your community unless your target audience is 30-something males.

Visits without Returns

Maybe you are getting visitors to your site, but they end up leaving without partaking in your expertise. In a way, this is positive news. It means your methods for getting exposure are working. But it also means that people are not buying what you are selling. If that is the case, you need to reevaluate your expertise, in terms of either learning more or finding a way to more effectively communicate what you know. Either way, you need to address the fact that customers are not seeing anything of value when they come to your site.

Visits without a Trace

If you attract visitors to your site but fail to get their e-mail addresses, you will have no way of reaching out to your community and no way of letting people know about the new products and services you are selling. Do not expect people to check in on your site regularly to see what you have to offer. Nobody has time—and that is why we have e-mail newsletters, RSS feeds, and other ways of pushing information out to people instead of waiting for them to come find it.[13]

Time

The tipping point will be different for everyone. For those needing traditional media to gain exposure, you are working at least six months behind people who can take advantage of blogs, user forums, and other technologies that are instantaneous. But that does not mean success will not happen. Unless your business is at a complete standstill, be patient, and put your efforts toward gaining exposure and fine-tuning your offering before abandoning the project.

In the old, closed model, if you wanted to pursue your passion, you had to start right here—at the advanced level of innovation. You had to decide immediately to start a business or abandon your dreams of getting compensated for your ideas, insights, and inventions. But in the open innovation model, going from idea to full-time business is meant to be evolutionary. As you increase your confidence and gain credibility at one level, you can stay where you are, scale back if it feels like too much, or step up your involvement if it feels right. Approach each step like an experiment. Have an idea and test it out. If it works, keep going. If it does not work, try something else. Continue this way until your North Star comes into focus and making money doing something you love becomes a reality.

---

[13]RSS stands for "Really Simple Syndication." Rather than having to go from blog site to blog site to check in on your favorite authors, you can set up an RSS feed so the blog contents come to you. It is a little like reading your e-mail inbox. Then you can just quickly go through the list of all the blogs you subscribed to and read the ones you are most interested in. Popular blog sites will have significantly more RSS subscribers than blog visitors, demonstrating that people want the content to come to them rather than the reverse. If you want to increase the number of people in your blog community, be sure it has RSS capability—the blog equivalent to capturing e-mail addresses on a traditional web site.

THREE EVERYDAY EXPERTS GET A MAKEOVER

PART 3: LEVERAGING THE PLATFORM

In Chapter 6, our everyday experts crafted a strategy for participating in the world of open innovation. Although they are still working in the intermediate level, they all have some ideas of how they would like to expand if and when the opportunity presents itself.

Kelly Hales, Dinner Club Expert

At the intermediate level, Kelly Hales plans to build an online resource to help other moms start their own dinner clubs. Because she does not have enough time to support a full-time business at this point in her life, she plans initially to build a web site for a small community of users. She will add content as time permits and will use word-of-mouth advertising exclusively. In the next few years, however, when she has more available time, she will actively engage a larger community of users, add forums and downloadable recipes, and perhaps even sell an e-book of dinner club recipes. The recipe book will be unique among all other recipe books because it will feature menus (not just individual dishes) and it will be geared toward feeding multiple families and creating food that can be easily portioned and transported.

Steve Collins, All-Star Basketball Academy Director

For years, Steve Collins has been teaching high school math and grooming talented athletes for play at the collegiate level. Though he makes very little money given all the hours spent in the gym, he truly enjoys what he is doing. With his new intermediate strategy for participating in open innovation, Collins is no longer perplexed about ways to make more money without moving up into upper-level coaching positions. Instead, he

(Continued)

is excited about finally finding a way to capitalize on his years of experience and culminating expertise.

Ironically, through the All-Star Academy, Collins is likely to be coaching players his high school team will ultimately face. Collins is okay with that predicament because although he is passionate about basketball, he would love nothing more than to help deserving kids get into good schools, further their education, and excel both on and off the court.

His plans to further monetize the All-Star Basketball Academy include possible geographic expansion into neighboring areas, adding downloadable training media to his web site, and potentially offering franchise opportunities across the country. The key for Collins will be to expand his geographic reach without having to spend too much time away from his family, which is one of the primary reasons he avoided moving to the college and professional levels of coaching in the first place.

Brooke Hall, Virtual Curb Adviser

Brooke Hall is actively working to learn blogging technology and create the templates she can use to help clients advertise their homes online. She is currently working full-time as a graphic artist while building her business on the side. When her Virtual Curb Appeal site reaches the potential to make more money than her current employment, she will transition into becoming a full-time entrepreneur.

While several of Hall's contemporaries are just starting out in the workforce, unsure of how they will make a living, Hall feels confident she is in a good position to take advantage of current and future technologies relevant to the real estate market. Since some industry gurus predict that real estate agents will eventually become extinct, Hall believes that helping people buy and sell their homes online, without a realtor, is not only an emerging trend but a necessary one.

PART THREE

FINE-TUNING YOUR EVERYDAY EXPERTISE

EIGHT

Be Good at Something: Pick a Niche, Fill a Need

Inventors approach me all the time with combination products—like a hammer that is also a screwdriver. But instead of getting a versatile tool, I am handed a lame hammer attached to an awkward screwdriver. So the consumer benefit of having two tools in one is negated by the fact that neither tool works very well at all. Good combination products are actually pretty rare. Most often, the blended products I see come from inventors who start off with mediocre ideas and then take the Ginsu knife approach to making it sound better than it really is. ("But wait, there's more! It can be a toy but it can also be used for camping!") I would rather see a product that does one thing well and solves a customer need than a mishmash product that serves no one in particular.

As you think about your everyday expertise, resist the urge to be a combination tool. Instead, pick something you are passionate about and do it better than anybody else. As you succeed in being number one in that niche, you can easily grow in other directions. If you start out too broad, however, you risk failing entirely.

Pick a Niche

My toy company (pre-Bendos craze) started out too general. We wanted to be an upscale, children's fantasy company—a brand parents could trust to deliver all things make-believe for their kids. We launched a catalog called Just Pretend and in it sold everything from dress-up costumes to puppets. Though we had a good idea of what products did and did not fit our model, consumers were confused. (Aren't all toys for pretend play?) Poor sales reflected the fuzzy message.

In hindsight, we should have focused on a product and a solution—like dress-up kits or something parents could buy to indulge their princesses without having to spend a king's ransom. If we had started the company with a clear point of distinction like that, we could have easily experimented and expanded into other make-believe products as the first one proved successful. However, we ended up backpedaling our brand and crafting a new message when, thankfully, Bendos took off.

Crocs, Inc., makers of those brightly colored resin shoes, did a much better job of starting in a niche market and letting their success lead the company into significantly bigger opportunities.[1] The rubber-like clog, originally marketed as a skidproof deck shoe for boating and other water sports, turned into a mainstream, multimarket phenomenon with Pet Rock type popularity. Boaters and other water people who first bought the shoe fell in love with Crocs' comfort and low-maintenance qualities (you can clean them with a garden hose, and the antibacterial substance prevents stinky foot odor). Those features then attracted a second breed of consumers—nurses, doctors, teachers, and other people who are on their feet all day. Well, who does not want comfortable shoes? As word of Crocs' unbelievable comfort and function spread, kids fell in line and their parents soon followed.

Now you can buy Crocs in a variety of styles and colors or pick from an array of licensed characters like Mickey Mouse, Batman, and Superman. You can even buy Crocs in your favorite college

---

[1] If you do not know what Crocs are, ask your kids or check out the Crocs web site at www.crocs.com.

team, Major League Baseball team, NASCAR team, National Football League team, and so forth. Growth has not been limited to just the shoes. The company also sells tiny decorations called Jibbitz so people can personalize their Crocs, and it recently expanded into other product categories like backpacks and customizable bags.

I doubt anyone at Crocs could have predicted the popularity these shoes have achieved. I would also bet that the company would not have done nearly as well if it had started out trying to sell the funny-looking shoes in as many places as it does now. But it managed to gradually infiltrate those markets by excelling at the original job of providing a comfortable, versatile shoe.

Like Crocs, do not start out as a generalist. Be a specialist. Excel in that narrow field and let the market pull you into broader arenas as your credibility increases. If you want to be an everyday expert on weddings, for example, a quick Google search will show that unless you want to compete with the two million other bridal experts already out there, you should refine your focus a little (or a lot). Instead, be the Hispanic bride's guide to getting married in Napa, or the do-it-yourself expert on nautical-themed weddings. When you become the number one provider in that category, you can expand your focus and use the positive reputation to spill over into broader markets.

CHALLENGE ASSUMPTIONS

When Rob McEwen introduced the Goldcorp challenge we talked about in Chapter 5, he awakened the fairly sluggish mining industry. That is what you have to do sometimes in order to find a strategic position. McEwen believes many people wake up in the morning with an idea but quickly talk themselves out of it by saying, "That doesn't relate to what I do and it's in another industry I know nothing about." By noon they forget about the idea altogether.

Having grown up in the financial industry, McEwen asked questions at GoldCorp that people in the company had never been asked before. He says, "Every business has fundamental assumptions that have never been questioned. If you can identify what those assumptions are and challenge them, you can identify alternatives that others in the industry will not be able to think of. Those alternatives can be developed into a strategic advantage and a competitive edge."

Fill a Need

Coming up with your area of specialty is one half of the equation. The other half is using your expertise to fill a consumer need. Although we tend to think of needs in terms of the products and services we would like to create, consumers think in terms of job requirements—what it is they are trying to accomplish. Then they buy various products and services to fulfill those jobs.

Think about the process of shopping for a kitchen gadget. You may set out looking for a new cheese grater, for example, but what you are really after is tiny bits of cheddar cheese on top of your chili. There are a variety of products you can hire to fill that need. You can use a fancy electric grater, the grater attachment for your food processor, a stand-alone metal grater with a rubber grip, a cheap plastic grater from the dollar bin, or one of the many other cheese shredders on the market. You could, however, simply buy pregrated cheese at the grocery store and skip the tools entirely. Or you could forgo cheese altogether and just eat the chili plain. There is always more than one way to meet a customer requirement. Your challenge is to be one of the best solutions available.

When I evaluate a new product or business, I look for two main customer touch points. The first is whether the innovation fundamentally makes the job simpler and more accessible to a larger number of people. Getting your teeth whitened is a good example of this. A few years ago, if you wanted whiter teeth, you had to look in the phone book to find a service, make a phone call, set up an appointment, get a consultation, and then hand over $700 to have a professional procedure done in an office. Not only did getting your teeth whitened take effort, but having someone look at your coffee-stained teeth was embarrassing, and paying several hundred dollars for a vanity procedure felt a little extravagant. Then along came the $30 in-home teeth-whitening kit you could buy at your local convenience store.

Getting your teeth whitened no longer requires an appointment. You can buy a home-use product fairly anonymously, nobody says the word "yellow" in front of you, and you put the goop on at night when it is convenient. Vanity is less of an issue because the cost of whitening your teeth is about the same price you would pay for a decent pedicure. Though the home kits probably do not work as well as the professional service dentists provide, the teeth-whitening market is suddenly a hundred times bigger and more accessible than it used to be.

The second touch point I look for in analyzing a new product or business is the emotional impact it will have on the consumer. I bought the iPhone primarily because of the functionality. But I also think it makes me look cool, and for a middle-aged father living in New Hampshire, that is important. People who buy compost bins do it so they can save money, recycle, and put enriched soil into their gardens. They also feel good about giving back to the earth. People hire party planners to offload the work of hosting a party. But they are also buying confidence that the event will be a hit.

As you develop your everyday expertise and seek to match it up with the needs of consumers, pay attention to how your business can address consumer touch points as well. As the Hispanic bride's guide to getting married in Napa, what exactly do your potential customers need from you? Do they need a bilingual wedding planner familiar with the Napa valley? Do they need resources for mariachi bands and Mexican caterers? Or are they looking for someone to create a celebration rich in familial traditions to make their grandparents proud?

The best way to find out what customers need from you is to ask. Whether you are interacting with consumers face-to-face or analyzing Web traffic and landing pages on your site, you want to start the feedback loop as soon as possible. Though you cannot implement every suggestion or please every person, look for patterns in the responses you get. ("This is the third Latina bride who has asked me where to find an ornate arras holder for the ceremony.") Then adapt your services to meet the repeated needs (i.e., find resources for places to buy the arras holders or sell them yourself).

The best way to find out why customers do *not* need you is also to ask. Why are they not interested in your product or service? Is there something you could be doing better? Are they landing on your blog but never once bothering to comment? Listen to their comments (and to their silence). You can decide later which suggestions to implement and which ones to ignore, but always start out by listening to see if the audience you are trying to reach understands what it is you are offering. If the message is blurry, like my "Just Pretend" scenario, then get more focused and experiment until you finally arrive at the magical crossroads where your everyday expertise fills a significant consumer need.

HOLD INFORMAL FOCUS GROUPS

Tracy Keough, managing director of O'Rorke, Inc., a social marketing company, recommends conducting focus groups and a number of one-on-one interviews with target customers at the ground floor of any project. She says that over the years, her most successful campaigns have been the result of companies understanding the opinions and attitudes of the target audience members before getting so entrenched in the issue, product, or service that they become blinded by their own objectives and miss discovering customers' realities. Although focus groups do not provide quantitative results, they can give much-needed insight into how potential customers really think and feel.

A focus group does not have to be formal or cost a lot of money. If, for example, you have a product or service you want to market to busy moms, invite several over to your house for a brunch and a quick gab session on the subject. Ask other moms at the park, or send an e-mail with a brief summary of your idea to friends in your son's playgroup.

When you do ask for input, tell people you are in the early stages and would appreciate honest feedback before investing further. Though friends may be reluctant to tell you that your idea stinks if the business has already been developed, they will probably give you candid feedback early on if they know doing so will save you future heartache.

EVERYDAY EXPERTS TALK ABOUT FINDING THEIR NICHE AND MEETING CUSTOMER NEEDS

Amie O'Shaughnessy, Owner of Ciao Bambino, Family-Friendly Travel Services[*]

As an entrepreneur, doing something new and unique can be nerve-racking because 50 percent of the people you talk to will tell you your idea is dumb and the other 50 percent will tell you it is brilliant. Listen to the people who are likely to be your future customers. Parents who wanted to travel with their children thought a family-friendly trip advisory service would be a huge success and encouraged the business. People without children or who had no desire to travel thought Ciao Bambino made absolutely no sense because they did not understand the customer need the service satisfies.

Weston Phillips, Five Point Productions, Winner of the Doritos Super Bowl Commercial Contest[†]

We knew the concept for the commercial would be the most important element of the production. So we brainstormed as a group for several hours, throwing everything up on the whiteboard, and working through a variety of ideas until we arrived at one story line that stood out among the rest. Ironically, some of

[*]www.ciaobambino.com.
[†]www.5pointproductions.com.

(Continued)

our early ideas showed up as concepts for some of the runner-up commercials we beat out. My advice is to recognize that there is always room for improvement in any one person's suggestion and that one idea, batted around, can spark even better ideas.

Nick Lindauer, Founder of Sweat 'N Spice and the Hot Sauce Blog*

Although our area of focus is a niche, we have not had to search that far to find other people interested in the same thing. In fact, the narrowness of our business is what makes the job interesting. We know all the bloggers on hot food topics, socialize with manufacturers and other professionals at big events and trade shows, and have even arranged to take trips with other hot sauce fanatics.

Jennifer Cosgrove, Greeting Card Universe Artist[†]

At Greeting Card Universe (GCU), we get statistics on store traffic, card clicks, popular keywords and so forth. I use that data to get a better idea of what cards work and what ones do not. For example, customized cards ("Happy Birthday Brother") sell faster than generic greetings do. Traditional jokes about age and getting older outperform edgier cards that only make a few people laugh. Not only can I use this data to increase sales at GCU, but it also helps me get a feel for what customers in other venues might be looking for.

Clifford Shakun, Creator of Designer Hospital Gowns

I had an idea to create designer hospital gowns so patients did not have to wear cheap, crappy clothing in their time of need. The idea seemed so simple, but nobody else was doing it.

---

*www.sweatnspice.com and www.hotsauceblog.com.

[†]Jennifer Cosgrove is a successful Greeting Card Universe artist. You can see her cards by typing "Cosgrove" in the "Search Cards" field on the Greeting Card Universe home page or you can go directly to her storefront at www.greetingcarduniverse .com/jencosgrove.

Now we sell anywhere from 1 to 1,000 gowns at a time and have marketed our products exclusively through Internet search engines and word-of-mouth referrals. A fortuitous mention in one of Google's marketing brochures put us on the world map, right in front of nearly everyone with a computer. We have managed to keep the top spots on our keywords for over seven years and have never looked back.*

*Keywords are the search terms that people use to find things on the Internet. Some of Shakun's keywords, for example, are "hospital gown" and "patient gown." You can use those keywords to quickly find Shakun's designer hospital gowns or you can go directly to his web site at www.hospitalgowns.com.

NINE

Invent for Less

T hroughout this book, I have talked interchangeably about product innovation and personal innovation (becoming an everyday expert). But I want to focus on the product side for a moment because many people falsely believe that inventing a product is a quick or easy way to become a millionaire. Although you can make a great deal of money inventing products, more often first-time inventors naively end up spending more money than they make. To profitably invent products, you must follow the same principles prescribed to the everyday expert: Think big, start small, find a niche, and fill a need.

Think Big, Start Small

Prototyping and patenting are two of the most misunderstood steps in the product development process. Conflicting theories in these areas often lead to confusion and unnecessary spending. I believe you should minimize expenses as much as possible so you will be receptive to feedback and responsive to changes that could improve the marketability of your product. And you should only consider investing more heavily in an invention when you are certain there is interest from consumers, retailers, or licensing companies. After all, the object is to cash checks, not write them!

Some say an invention needs to be production-ready, down to the trademarked name and clamshell packaging, before showing it to potential clients so that there is little need to use the imagination when reviewing the product. While I agree that it is easier to envision a product's potential when you can hold it in your hand, I disagree that you should complete development before seeking feedback and potential interest. If you wait until a product is done (in your mind) and have already invested heavily in getting it there, you are more likely to be defensive when improvements are suggested.

Arra David, for example, submitted a prototype invention called the Craft Lite Cutter to the office supply hunt we ran for Staples a few years ago. The Craft Lite Cutter is a rotary-style paper trimmer with a light under the cutting surface to backlight the paper and make cuts more accurate. It also has a variety of interchangeable blades that enable users to create a zigzag, scallop, or other ornamental edge with a simple swipe of the handle. Although Staples did not select the product, we loved its potential. With David's permission, we showed the prototype to Merchant Media, Inc., which licensed the product in its rough, prototype form.[1]

For the next year, however, Merchant Media, BIG, and the inventor worked together to refine the prototype and get feedback from potential customers. During that time, we made several important discoveries that improved the product's overall potential. First we replaced the original bulb lighting mechanism with two LED lights. This change reduced the weight of the product and improved its durability because LED lights last longer and use less battery power than conventional bulbs. Next, we changed the industrial size cutting surface to a smaller one with a flip-out ruler to make the product portable and more appealing to crafters.

In carrying around that new version of the product, we discovered that the cutting disks could be neatly stored on the cutter

[1]Arra David is a designer and an engineer. I love getting product ideas from David because he generally works out some of the major design flaws before we even see the product. But not everybody has an engineering background or accessibility to the tools David has. Popsicle stick prototypes are just as welcome as the professional looking ones. Some of David's other creations include the Hoverbench (www.hoverbench.com), the Spira mailbox (www.spiramailbox.com) and Sea Stones (www.sea-stones.com). The Craft Lite Cutter can be seen (and ordered!) from www.craftlitecutter.com.

handle, eliminating the need to develop and manufacture a separate disk storage device as originally planned. We also got surprising feedback from experienced crafters that prompted a change in the marketing strategy. The original prototype did not have the decorative cutting blades and we thought crafters would see the ability to cut a deadly accurate straight line as the primary benefit. Although they liked that feature, they loved the versatility and assortment of the decorative blades even more. So we moved that benefit to the top of our selling points.

Because we minimized expenses and routinely sought feedback from potential users, we managed to incorporate these changes and a variety of others that ultimately reduced the product's cost and improved its design, packaging, and marketing message. Merchant Media ended up with a better end product, and we all got reassurances that consumers would embrace this new invention thanks to positive feedback during the trial phase.[2]

Do not rush through or bypass this critical experimental stage. An idea should go from your head to a piece of paper—write it down and sketch it up in some form. Then ask people about it. I often have inventors show up at BIG Roadshows with nothing more than a notebook full of ideas, no more developed than a bunch of drawings on paper. I am not going to grab something out of the book and license it, but I am happy to sift through the various ideas and help a person figure out which ones to take to the next level. But you do not need my help to do that. Start with your friends and family. If you get an initial nod of approval on your idea and nobody comes up with any obvious objections, then incorporate the changes that make sense and ask potential customers for their feedback. I even suggest asking retailers what they think. If you have a new cell phone accessory, for example, go to the   Verizon and Sprint kiosks in the mall and see what those folks think about it.

If you still think the idea has merit, move to the three-dimensional phase. But do not open the yellow pages and start looking for an industrial designer or a machinist. Instead, get out the cardboard,

[2]Merchant Media is another infomercial giant. We like licensing products to infomercial companies because they do large-volume sales, which means nice, fat royalty checks.

ASKING FOR FEEDBACK

I know it can take courage to ask people what they think of your ideas. But the quicker you learn to avoid emotional reactions to positive and negative feedback, the sooner you will be able to save or make money based on the input you receive. Rather than asking people if they love or hate your idea, however, explain the problem you are trying to solve and ask probing questions to learn more and to make the process less personal. Here are a few suggestions:

- Have you ever experienced a similar problem?
- What products have you tried to address the problem?
- Is the problem that big of a deal to you? (In other words, would you pay money to have it solved?)
- How well do you think this invention would solve the problem?
- What changes would you make to this product?
- What features would you add?
- What features are of no value to you and should be removed?
- How much would you expect to pay for something like this?
- Where would you expect to buy a product like this?

play dough, and duct tape. Make something. Ask for feedback. Go to Home Depot and buy inexpensive products you can hack apart and glue together to make an even better prototype. Then ask for more feedback. Local schools are also a great resource for help getting your product into a working three-dimensional version: Talented design students will do some amazing work just to build up their portfolios—sometimes for a piece of the royalties, sometimes for just a few slices of pizza.

As the invention becomes more lifelike and your confidence in consumer interest for the end product increases, you can inch your way toward hiring professionals to make better prototypes if needed. You can also start thinking about talking to a patent attorney. Information protection (IP) is another potential money pit for inventors because they think getting a patent is one of the first steps in the product development process. For me, it is closer to the bottom of the list. I only invest in IP when I am fairly certain I have a buyer. Though a patent can be expensive, it can provide important protection, and I take the step knowing I will very likely recover the costs if the product makes it to market.

Some web sites say you can reduce the cost of inventing by writing your own patent and filing your own IP applications. That is only a good approach if you have a bad idea. But if you have gone through the iterative process of prototyping, refining, and incorporating feedback into your design and still have something people are interested in, then writing your own patent is like reading a book on how to cut hair and then pulling out the scissors to give yourself a trim. Your hair will eventually grow back out. Do-it-yourself IP work, however, can have longer-lasting ill effects if you fail to aggressively cover the important aspects of your invention, making it easier for others to legally copy or improve upon your product.

Instead of doing your own IP work to save money, wait until all manufacturing and development issues have been worked out before starting the patent process. If you start too early, you risk having to redo the patent application to incorporate discoveries (that costs money). And do your homework ahead of time so that when you do finally sit down with an attorney, you can make efficient use of the time (fewer billable hours).

Homework includes researching similar inventions found online, in stores, and in the U.S. Patent and Trademark Office's online database of issued patents and pending applications.[3] Information about competitive products can help the attorney decide how to protect

---

[3]The best way to access this database is to go to the main web site at www.uspto.gov, select "Patents" and then select "Search Patents" in the left-hand menu.

PARANOIA WILL DESTROY AN IDEA

In order to really seek feedback from others, you need to get over the paranoia that the people you talk to are going to steal your ideas. My experience is that inventing takes too much work and people are too busy leading their normal lives to take on the abnormal work of trying to rip you off. Trust me. The clerk at Best Buy is not going to run home and start inventing his own version of the cable organizer you just showed him. One inventor I met refused to show his invention to anyone, including his wife. "Well how can someone decide if they want to license it?" I asked. He responded, "They need to trust me that it is worth at least a million dollars." Okay. Next please. If you are still concerned, however, here are a few ways to protect your ideas without spending any real money:

- Get an inventor's notebook and document your idea. You do not need a fancy book called an "Inventor's Note-book." One of those cheap black-and-white composition books will do just fine. For information about how to document your work, read about inventor's notebooks on Wikipedia.

- Before you talk to people about your idea, explain that you are doing so in confidence and would appreciate their discretion in keeping it to themselves. Most people will do that. Professionals will especially do that because they know a breach of confidence is unethical and they do not need the negative publicity of being sued.

- If you are really concerned, have people sign a nondisclosure agreement (NDA). You can find resources for confidentiality agreements at Nolo.com (www.nolo.com) and at IPWatchdog.com (www.ipwatchdog.com).

your invention and whether it is worth the effort to try. Be prepared to talk about the various prototypes and discoveries that prompted improvements. These variations may not be in the preferred version of your product, but can be included in the IP protection to make your patent stronger. And brainstorm other uses for your product as well. Though we want to stay focused on the main use of your invention when putting it on the market, documenting alternative uses in a patent is another way to make IP stronger. But do not confuse an investment in IP as a way of making money.

Information protection can be one of the tools to help you make money and can be used as a barrier to competition, but it is not a requirement. Many inventions get licensed or put on the market without any IP at all. And thoughtful work such as a good design, developing a strong brand, and being the first to fill a niche can thwart competition as well. So think extensively about the costs and benefits of IP before pulling out your wallet.

Prototyping and patenting are two of the most difficult areas for inventors to navigate without wasting money. But if inventing a product is part of your North Star vision, I am certainly not here to hold you back. In fact, I want you on my A-list of inventors. But I would rather you get there through inexpensive experimentation and learning than costly mistakes and sob stories.

Pick a Niche, Fill a Need

People bring me an awful lot of inventions pertaining to the bathroom—ways to make the toilet paper unravel easier, antiodor devices, disposable bidets, and a variety of other products that I am just not sure the public is quite ready to see. Although you could argue that we must have a need for innovation in that area, I think we get a proliferation of potty products because people are quite reflective while sitting on the throne. Unfortunately, not all of these inspirations are worth pursuing and the existing products are actually pretty darn good. In fact, most of the inventions in this area should be *in* the toilet.

Another problematic area for new inventors is coming up with truly innovative ideas. I see a great number of me-too product ideas from people who think they can make small improvements or cosmetic changes to something already on the market and either start a business around it or get another company to pay them a royalty. But it takes a little more work than that, and investing your money in something so insignificant can be a waste. Even if your stuffed puppy in a handbag is cuter than the one already on sale at Target, buyers are not likely to switch from their existing supplier just because the pink and brown buttons on your bag are cuter than the blue ones already on the shelf.

TEN HABITS OF HIGHLY EFFECTIVE INVENTORS

I have met thousands of inventors over the years, ranging from the moms who turn their minds loose on problem-solving ideas while sitting alongside splashing toddlers in the bathtub, to the industrial designers who have spent years perfecting other people's ideas and now want to profit from some of their own. In working with these creative individuals, I see the best ideas and greatest opportunity for success come from those who do the following things:

1. They keep a notebook, folder, or drawer full of ideas. Every idea is worth considering; nothing is eliminated immediately. The repository of ideas is always growing.

2. They let ideas marinate in their heads before rushing off to the patent attorney or the workshop.

3. They work well with partners or other inventors. Good ideas are often turned into great ideas when put in front of other creative people, particularly those with strengths complementary to the inventor.

4. They do their homework. They are expert at searching the Internet, stores, and prior patents for similar ideas.

5. Their concepts evolve. A good problem can be solved in many ways and the first solution is not always the best solution. As inventors develop prototypes, seek input, and do research, they incorporate what they learned or reroute and revise the original concept.

6. They are good salespeople. They are passionate about their ideas, and that enthusiasm shows when they make a pitch.

7. They are persistent. When one experiment fails, they pull another idea out of the notebook and try again.

8. They are versatile. They have trained their minds to creatively problem-solve and can apply that insight to ideas for kitchenware, kids' snacks, sporting gear, and beyond.

9. They let go. They do not spend years tinkering, dwelling, and holding on to their one big idea. They experiment, learn, improve, sell, and know when to walk away.

10. They enjoy the process. Inventing takes work, and the percentage of ideas that ultimately make money is small. But effective inventors thrive on the creative exercises and the glimmer of hope that the next idea might actually be the big one.

Big companies have smart people working every day to think of improvements or extensions to their existing product lines. These guys are going to think of the easy stuff like adding wheels to the cooler, creating designer skins for the iPod, putting Ziploc closures on the chip bag, and making silicone oven mitts to go with the existing silicone bakeware. So do not waste your time working on the obvious things these companies have likely already tried or are currently exploring. Search for easy solutions to really annoying problems instead.

Train your mind to focus on solving a problem that has no good solution or thinking of new and clever alternatives to a problem that has been solved in inferior ways. Prior to the invention of the

SpinBrush, for example, you had to buy an expensive electric toothbrush in order to get the dental benefit of a rotating brush head. But then an independent inventor designed a disposable, battery-operated, rotating brush that costs less than a cappuccino. Procter & Gamble bought the technology from the inventor and relaunched the product as the Crest SpinBrush, now one of the top-selling automated toothbrushes on the market.

Now do not run off and start sketching the SpinFloss idea that just popped into your head, thinking you can piggyback on the SpinBrush's success. Guaranteed, several other people at P&G have already considered it. But I would like you to think about extensions of your own product ideas. When Vanessa McGarry and Paige Snear Apar brought us the "Fun with Food" concept, for example, I liked their big-picture vision. The two had recently licensed the automatic Twirling Spaghetti Fork to Hog Wild and wanted to show me similar ideas.[4]

Conventional etiquette says children should not play with their food. But McGarry and Apar pitched the concept that moms struggle to get kids to sit at the table and eat without being nagged. So they created a line of products giving kids permission to twirl their spaghetti noodles and put their fingers in the veggies, making dinnertime less of a chore for the whole family.

Manufacturers and retailers are always interested in product and brand potential. Start small, of course, with an innovative idea and a simple prototype. But have some ideas about where the product can go on its own (different sizes, uses, materials, and so forth) and how it could fit within an entire line of products (utensils, dishes, and servings trays that change colors according to the temperature of the food). Then pitch your product idea within the context of the bigger story so potential customers can visualize evolving sales possibilities.

---

[4]The Twirling Spaghetti Fork works like the SpinBrush only there are metal prongs on the end of it instead of a brush. If that does not make sense, look at it on the Hog Wild web site at www.hogwildtoys.com. Incidentally, Hog Wild is an inventor-friendly company, meaning they welcome ideas from people outside of the company. In this case, however, they would like to see prototypes to be sure your product really works before they invest in further developing it.

And finally, when you do get the chance to meet with a manufacturer or a retail buyer, take the opportunity to listen and learn. I have walked into many offices with a portfolio full of products to show and walked back out with zero in sales but a fortune in valuable information. Approach every meeting as a chance to get feedback and find out more about the company's needs. Are they looking to solve a specific problem? Are they looking for products to pit against a competitor's goods? If they could describe an ideal product, what would it be? Then work diligently to develop innovative ideas to match the requirements you have been given. Though you can certainly invent products born out of your own needs, you are more likely to succeed as an inventor if you think about your customers' needs instead.

SUCCESSFUL INVENTORS WEIGH IN

Arra David, Inventor of the Craft Lite Cutter

Many people come up with ideas they think are totally original only to later discover that not only has somebody thought of it before, but they got the patent on it before you were even born. I have learned the hard way that the first few hours after coming up with a new idea are best spent looking online to see if it already exists rather than running straight to the workshop to build a prototype. Do a Google search to see if it is on the market and then spend time researching patents on Google Patents and the U.S. Patent and Trademark Office web site (www.uspto.gov).

I also recommend finding an inventor organization in your area. Not only can you network with other inventors and find more ways to invent without spending a fortune, but you can also get referrals for trusted professionals such as industrial engineers, patent attorneys, marketing specialists, and so forth when the time comes. I belong to the Inventors Association of New England but you can find a group in your area by

(Continued)

selecting "Listing of Inventor Groups" on the United Inventors Association web site (www.uiausa.com).

Paige Snear Apar and Vanessa McGarry, Inventors of the Twirling Spaghetti Fork

The best way to save money inventing is to license your invention to a company who will do all the grunt work of manufacturing, shipping, and so forth and pay you a royalty for each product sold. To attract potential licensors, first create a good visual of your idea. Get a copy of Adobe Photoshop and learn how to create your own images and diagrams to save the cost of hiring a graphic artist. Do not make an expensive prototype, but do research the best materials and technology for your concept. Some people invest several thousand dollars in a prototype only to discover a simple drawing with specifications would have sufficed.

Roger Brown, Inventor of the Quick Clip and Several Other Products[*]

To be successful, you need persistence to work through the down times and still keep a creative spirit. You need patience to go through the hurry-up-and-wait phase of your submissions and not ruin the chances of licensing your product by being a pest. You need a positive attitude in an industry that will give you more rejections than yeses. And you need to be able to take criticism and look at your ideas from the point of the company receiving it, not just your own objectives of wanting to get it to market.

---

[*]Roger Brown is a serial inventor and a cartoonist. He is a regular in the Inventor Spot forum (www.inventorspot.com), a great resource for any new inventor. You can see Brown's licensed products and his artwork on www.rogerbrown.net.

Barbara Russell Pitts and Mary Russell Sarao, Inventors of Ghostline Products[*]

While a wonderful new invention can create a fabulous income stream for years to come, the financial prospect of getting from idea to market can be daunting. Successful independent inventors on a budget pay *only* for what they cannot do themselves. Do your own market search and preliminary patent search. Create your first prototype and prove it works using inexpensive materials. Pay only for the information protection you need as it aligns with your plans for the product. And avoid being scammed by invention submissions firms with slick advertising and flashy promises.

Kim Babjak, Inventor of Zip-A-Ruffle[†]

I started my business with $300, most of that going toward business cards and a fax machine so I could work with QVC. I asked my family members for any extra office equipment they had and managed to round up a desk, a file cabinet, and a fake plant. I also bartered a great deal and volunteered my time in exchange for services. When I couldn't afford the cost of a seminar that I really wanted to attend, for example, I volunteered to work the event so I could listen to the speaker.

---

[*]If you have ever tried to write on plain poster board, then you will applaud when you see Pitts and Sarao's invention. Ghostline products have a "ghosted" grid that makes it easier than ever to write in a straight line across a poster. Learn more about these prolific inventors on their web site, www.asktheinventors.com or buy a copy of their self-published book, *Inventing on a Shoestring Budget* for several more money-saving tips.

[†]The Zip-A-Ruffle is a bed skirt that zips on and off for easy cleaning. Search for Zip-A-Ruffle on the QVC web site (www.qvc.com) and see more of what Babjak is doing on her web site (www.kimcoaz.com).

TEN

Sink or Swim: Learn How to Sell

T he guidelines for product submissions to BIG are pretty lenient in terms of how far an idea needs to be developed before we will see it. Some inventors come in with pencil sketches or computer-aided design (CAD) drawings while others bring in three-dimensional models ranging from homemade prototypes to tricked-out, professionally manufactured samples. But amidst all those who bring in products at various stages of development are several others who walk through the doors with inventory ready to sell. When I ask these inventors what they need me for (after all, they have done most of the hard work), invariably the answer is, "I need help selling."

The problem most people have with sales is that they view the task in a derogatory context, like a pushy used-car salesman or a telemarketer who interrupts dinner. And because they do not want to appear like those people, they either sell passively (build a web site and hope people find it, or tell family members and hope they spread the word) or skip the exercise entirely. The result is boxes full of inventory sitting in a garage, and wasted time and money put toward building a business that will never come to fruition.

It is very hard to do well as an entrepreneur if you do not change this mind-set because nearly every type of business, in one way or another, requires sales. Whether you are selling a product or a service to a consumer, asking other bloggers to link to your blog, pushing people to vote for your designs, or enticing people to sign up for your newsletter, you need to be able to talk confidently about what it is you are offering in order to get people to take action. So if you want to be successful in your new venture, get over the sales stigma and either learn how to sell or partner with someone else who does.

Get Over the Stigma

For many people, *selling* implies getting someone to buy something they neither want nor need, like when you go to the concession stand at the movie theater to buy a small popcorn and return to your seat carrying a jumbo bucket and two drinks (even though you are at the movies alone). But selling can be quite the opposite, like helping someone find a solution to their problem, a way to save money, a product that performs better than the one they had in mind, a referral to a service they did not know existed, and so forth. If you focus on positive sales experiences (when someone listened to your needs and helped you find a solution) rather than negative ones (when you bought something and later felt suckered), you are more likely to feel good about learning how to sell.

In fact, the best salespeople are those who learn to listen first and sell second. Rather than pushing your agenda on people, ask them what they need. People will happily talk about their pain points and problem areas. If they do happen to mention something you can help with, then you have the perfect opening to pitch your products, services, or know-how as an answer to their problem. If not, ask more questions. Sometimes a match between a customer need and your solution only surfaces after more in-depth conversation. Likewise, you might uncover an opportunity to innovate something new and wonderful.

I have talked at length about BIG's transition from toy company to consumer product company, from licensing agent to Hunt sponsor, from Hunt club to Insight Clubs, and so forth. All of these evolutions came as a result of talking with clients who expressed needs I could not fill. But I took the information, went back to the office, developed a solution, and returned to these clients with a way to address their problem. They were happy, of course, and I got to expand my business in a way I had not previously considered.

Sales, done right, can be a good experience for all parties.

Learn How to Sell

A new middle school opened up in our area so my wife and I took the kids over for a tour. We were all excited to walk around the brand-new building, see the classrooms, and check out the gym. But after only a few minutes of following behind a tour guide who mumbled and lacked any real enthusiasm for the school, I wanted to ditch the excursion and come back later on our own. We suffered through the evening anyway.

But all the way home, I lectured my kids on projecting confidence. And I will say the same to you: To be good at sales, you not only need to listen, but you also need to be able to speak confidently about what it is you are selling. And the best way to get confident is to study the subject matter, develop an elevator pitch, and practice.

SET YOURSELF UP FOR SUCCESS

Selling your new product, service, or everyday expertise can be a little daunting if getting started requires physically networking with people such as cold-calling, attending business mixers, knocking on doors, talking to strangers in the elevator, and so on. But here are a few ways to make it easier on yourself before you even start:

- Pick a good business name, one that is easy to say and gives some indication of what you are all about. If you name the business "LBR, Inc." after the initials of your three kids, you will spend an inordinate amount of time explaining what the company name stands for and what it is you do. Use descriptive words instead like The Grout Guru, Nacho Cheese Universe, or Beauty Expert for Busy Moms.

- Get an inexpensive business card. Not only can you use the card as a conversation starter about your new venture, but it also tells people you are serious about doing it.

- Create an inexpensive leave-behind of some sort such as a sell sheet, a list of services, or background information. Hand this to prospective clients, but do not expect them to read it in front of you. (It is called a leave-behind for a reason). Instead, talk face-to-face while you can and leave the material behind as you exit.

- Create an online presence. Whether you set up a one-page web site or a MySpace account, having a place on the Internet makes it significantly easier for people to find out more about you or your business after the initial conversation has ended. And people are much more likely to remember how to contact you later if you refer them to a web site address rather than a telephone number ("Check me out at GroutGuru.com").

Study the Subject Matter

The more you know about a subject, the more confident you will be when discussing it. A friend of mine noticed that several inventors moved quickly through the prototyping phase of developing their ideas, only to stagnate when faced with the task of cold-calling and trying to license their inventions. So she started a business to help inventors get over this hurdle. For a flat rate, she would develop a sell sheet for the product and research potential licensors in the industry. Then she would give the marketing material and research packet back to the inventor, thinking he would then pick up the phone and start contacting the recommended companies.

But she quickly realized that her clients were just as scared to sell their inventions after getting the data as they had been beforehand. Having hired out the research of thinking through a product's benefits, looking for players in the industry, and identifying market opportunities, the inventors inadvertently bypassed the personal growth and confidence that comes from working through the process on their own.

Even though I am pretty self-assured when it comes to representing products, I still do my homework before meeting with any new client. I do not, however, profess to have all the answers. If I am asked a question I cannot answer, I admit not knowing and promise to follow up after the meeting.

Develop an Elevator Pitch

An elevator pitch is a concise (30 to 60 seconds) way of explaining in everyday terms what you do, who you do it for, and why it is interesting and unique. Because, in theory, you have just a brief moment to convince someone to take your business card before getting off the elevator, every word in the speech should be chosen carefully and practiced until it can be said confidently, even when you are nervous.

In addition to explaining your business, the elevator speech can help generate excitement for what you are doing. No matter where you are in the process of starting your business, talk about the success you are already having. For example, "We have over 3,000 blog subscribers"; "We are already the second largest organic clothing manufacturer in Oregon"; "Everybody who has tested the product loves it." (Who cares if your mom and sister are the only ones who have tried it? They both liked it, so that makes "everybody.")

And finally, use the elevator speech to solicit further interaction. Ask for a meeting to continue the conversation. Invite them to subscribe to your newsletter to learn more. Encourage attendance at a workshop you are giving. Or suggest a follow-up phone call to discuss possible opportunities together.

Practice

In addition to practicing your elevator pitch, you should also try just selling something—anything. A good way to gain sales confidence is to sell for someone else. Work in the snack bar at the Little

League field, volunteer to help at the school's fund-raising auction, or man a booth at the church carnival. It does not matter what you sell. What matters is that you will get better at talking to strangers, asking what they need, and seeing if you have a way to fill it. You will also get experience looking for opportunities (e.g., more than 10 customers asked if we had sprinkles to put on top of the ice cream).

SAMPLE ELEVATOR SPEECHES

For my company:

> Big Idea Group does innovation projects for major companies. We do innovation research with online communities of actual consumers, and we do innovation hunts where companies use our network of 12,000 people to innovate new products. We've run dozens of projects and helped create over 60 new products and services with this approach. We also start a new innovative start-up company almost every year, based on our work.

For the Craft Lite Cutter:

> With traditional paper cutters, it is very hard to cut exactly where you want. You guess, and either slice the good stuff or nibble your way in, which takes forever. The Craft Lite Cutter gives you a visible cutting line, so you cut exactly where you want to cut every time. It also has an array of blades to make cutting decorative edges easier than ever. The product has tested fantastically well and is being launched nationally via infomercial.

For a genealogy everyday expert:

> Everyone wants to know more about their family history, but not everybody has the time or the know-how to research it. I do personalized genealogy for families, focusing on personal stories and events, rather than dates and places. We are also experimenting in medical genealogy. For example, I discovered a family that had a history of appendicitis. When the mother came down with appendicitis symptoms, she was aware she could be susceptible and went in right away to have her appendix removed.

GETTING THE MEETING

Not all of the businesses we are talking about require physically prospecting for customers. But for those that do, asking for a meeting can be one of the most terrifying steps in the sales process. Here are a few tricks to ease any anxieties you might have.

- Figure out what you need to say and write it down. The prospecting conversation is similar to the elevator speech in that you need to briefly explain the benefits of your product or service in everyday language and add an element of intrigue. Then you need to ask for the meeting. For example, "I have a working prototype of a wireless mouse that is smaller than a golf ball but is still ergonomically correct. I let 20 programmers in my office test it out and 80 percent said they would buy one tomorrow if they could. When would be a good time for me to show it to you?"

- Practice the call with someone else. A perfectly crafted pitch on paper can end up sounding like a monologue when you finally get the person on the phone. So try it out beforehand and ask for feedback.

- Once you do have the pitch perfected, practice saying it over and over again until it comes out naturally.

- Follow the same steps with potential questions the person you are calling might ask. Being prepared for hesitation ("We do not usually meet with outside inventors"), rejection ("No thanks"), or more probing questions ("Can you tell me more about it first?") can help you keep the confident facade from crumbling if the conversation veers from what you expect.

- Take a deep breath. Pick up the phone and dial. Although it can be tempting to leave a message on voice mail, taking the easy way out is not likely to get the results you desire.

Call back later toward the end of the day or in the early morning hours before the receptionist arrives. Executives are more likely to answer their own phone during that time.

- Each time you call, make a point to befriend the operator and sweet-talk the assistant. Though they are paid to act as gatekeepers, deflecting nuisance calls and redirecting cold-callers, these people can turn into your biggest allies if you are professional and courteous every time you call. They might even put in a good word for you or tip you off on best times to call back.

- When you do finally get the chance to set up a meeting, be brief and accommodating. I never ask for more than a few minutes and I try to be as flexible as possible. "I can tell you about our services in about 15 minutes. I'll be respectful of your time and I'll meet wherever it is convenient for you. Would Thursday at 11:00 work?"

The First Sale

Getting that first customer can be the hardest because until you do, you do not have a sales history to boast about or satisfied customers to quote. In the early days of starting a business, I suggest you be very giving, even to the point of giving something away for free.

Art Fry, inventor of 3M's Post-it Notes, often tells the story of how the product tested horribly and almost got abandoned in the early days because consumers did not understand how to use the sticky notes. So the company took a truckload of Post-its to a single market in the Northwest and gave the inventory away. Not only did people love the notes, but they found a zillion uses for them. Fry swears the Post-it Note success never would have happened had they not done the sampling program.

You do not have to give away a truckload of anything. But be creative and figure out what you can afford to volunteer. If you are starting a new party service, for example, offer to throw a free party for someone. But be strategic. Offer the complimentary party to someone who will spread the word among other potential customers, such as a well-networked mom in an affluent community or a preschool teacher who will invite all the kids in the classroom.

In exchange for the free service, ask for feedback, pictures for your portfolio, and a testimonial for your marketing material. Use that information to make adjustments if needed (e.g., people loved the party but thought the suggested price quoted to the hostess was too high).

MAKING THE MOST OF THE MEETING

You finally got the meeting. Congratulations! Now make the most of it by following this advice:

- Dress professionally and arrive on time.
- Be overly nice to the receptionist, especially if she helped you get the meeting. Not only will your paths cross again if the company has an interest in what you are selling, but she might be brought into the meeting for one reason or another and it is best to keep her on your good side. I often bring others into my office when an inventor shows me an idea that I think someone else would have an interest in. If you blow past those people in a hurry to meet me, you might face a tough crowd when I ask them to join us for a few minutes.
- Do your homework prior to the meeting. Study the industry, know the gaps in the market, and be prepared to discuss where your products or services fit. Taking the time to gather this information will help build your confidence. That confidence will be evident in the meeting.
- Listen. Before you launch into the pitch, start by asking the person what it is they need. If you have done your homework, then you probably already have a good sense of what they are going to say. If you are right, then they

have provided you with a perfect segue into the benefits you can provide. If you are not right, then you have learned some valuable information instead.

- Be yourself and just talk. Ditch the technical jargon; it does not make you sound smarter. Hand out background material, but do not expect people to read it while you are there. Have your note cards handy in case you get nervous, but do not plan to read them either. Just speak from your experiences. What led you to this idea? What problem were you faced with? Why do you think others will be interested in your solution? I have put many tongue-tied inventors at ease by asking them to drop the formalities and just tell me about the problem they are solving and how they came up with the solution.

- Follow up. Every deal has a half-life. In order to capitalize on the meeting, you need to move forward within days. I typically wait just 48 hours before making the first follow-up call. If I do not get a response to that call, I wait another 48 hours and try again. Then I drop the waiting period to 24 hours. Then 12 hours. Then I call every hour until I get some sort of an answer.

Get Someone Else to Help

Sometimes it is just easier to sell something you are not personally invested in. So I would rather you surrender and ask for help in the sales department then abandon your dreams entirely because you just cannot get past your anxieties. We all have our strengths and weaknesses. To survive as an everyday expert, you need to figure out what areas you excel in and what areas you need help with. Though you can discount some aspects of the business and wait to improve them later, such as adding better graphics to your web site or getting business cards printed at FedEx Kinkos instead of at home, sales is not an aspect you can afford to ignore.

SALES EXPERTS GIVE ADVICE

Stephen Key, Inventor and Co-Founder of inventRight[*]

People need to understand that the mood they are in will come right through the phone. So you need to have a positive attitude and be in the frame of mind that what you are selling is fun, interesting, and something the person on the other end will want. If you have a hard time getting into that mind-set, fake it until it feels authentic.

To really build confidence on the phone, however, you need to believe in what you are selling. A great way to build that confidence is to test the product out on a small scale. For example, when we first started developing Hot Picks (designer guitar picks), I took samples to a music store and paid the guy behind the counter to hand out free picks to any guitarist willing to provide feedback and fill out a questionnaire. Not only did the artists love the picks, but their comments were fantastic and very insightful. The positive responses fueled our enthusiasm for the project, gave us great testimonials to quote, and boosted our self-assurance every time we picked up the phone.

David Porter, Co-Inventor of the FURminator deShedding Tool[†]

Although we ultimately planned to sell our invention to consumers in general, we really felt like we needed to start out selling the product to trade professionals to establish

---

[*]In his inventRight seminars, Stephen Key also warns inventors to save their money by creating prototypes on their own and getting the licensing company to pay for information protection. Key also advocates having a "benefit statement," which is similar to the elevator speech. You can learn more at www.inventright.com.

[†]The FURminator de-Shedding Tool demonstration on QVC is fantastic. You see this dog on the stage and as they start the process, piles and piles of hair fall to the ground. Who would not buy the product after that powerful visual? You can see a similar demonstration on www.furminator.com.

(Continued)

credibility. First we hit all the grooming trade shows. Then we expanded our marketing to include veterinarians and other professionals who would benefit from the product's capabilities. Success in those fields eventually led us to QVC, where we became the most successful selling pet product in the show's history.

Laura Cunitz, Founder of Bella Knitting[*]

Encourage others to thrive within your environment and within the industry you are working in. People who license products to Bella Knitting, for example, turn into virtual inside sales representatives for the company. They are excited about making money from the projects they licensed to us and, as a result, talk about their success in other forums, blogs, web sites, and even traditional knitting communities. Our sales increase from the additional exposure and their royalties increase because we sell more of their products. All parties benefit in the exchange.

Scott Holstein, Owner of Kim & Scott's Gourmet Pretzels[†]

Retailers want the type of innovative products they can get from smaller manufacturers but need the reliability and

---

[*] Even though Cunitz uses her blog to promote her knitting projects web site, her style is so friendly and informal that you do not feel like you are being sold anything. She never says, "Go to my web site and buy our new cardigan project." Instead, she says something subtle like, "I'm thinking about cables today because we just completed a really great sweater for fall that has cabling down the sleeves." The narrative is then followed by a link to the project on her web site at www.bellaknitting.com. If you use this technique, be sure the link takes you directly to the sweater referenced—not to the home page, leaving the person wondering where the sweater is.

[†] Though the Holsteins of Kim & Scott's Pretzels (www.kimandscotts.com) met with the QVC buyer along with hundreds of other people trying to get their products on QVC, the Holsteins were not nervous. They joked around, ate pretzels, and had fun with the buyers. I am sure that helped get them a spot on QVC since selling the product yourself is often part of the deal. If you cannot talk passionately about your product to three people, how can you expect to reach 30 million?

service they can get from larger manufacturers. They cannot afford to take a risk and place a large order with a small company that might not deliver or be able to increase an order if sales go well. So retailers will typically stick with suppliers who are safe. One way to overcome this hesitancy is to ensure all of your marketing materials look professional. You do not need a large quantity or need a lot of different materials, just be sure that what you do have demonstrates quality. Another suggestion is to get a third-party (another customer or your supplier, for example) to vouch for you. And if that fails, try acting as a private-label supplier until your company builds enough credibility in the industry to create products under your own brand.

ELEVEN

Get Over It: Learn from Rejection

I have had many business successes; I have also had my share of failures. I have had business ideas turned down, funding requests denied, products that retailers would not put on their shelves, inventions nobody wanted to license, employees who quit, and a myriad of other disappointing experiences. But I have learned through the years that from each negative event comes an opportunity to gain knowledge. I also believe that if you have not had a good share of failures, you probably have not tried anything very interesting. Just as you cannot escape learning how to sell, if you want to chase your dreams and find a way to make money doing something you love, you will need to brace yourself for the inevitable rejections that will come.

My professional dream—my North Star—is creating innovative products, services, and businesses, working with like-minded people, and doing it on my terms, including with whom, what, when, and where I want to work. Pretty lofty vision, eh? Maybe, but I did not get here in one big gesture. I tried out various ideas, winning on some and losing on others, learning every step of the way, until eventually I achieved this goal on some level. (I am always reaching higher, of course.)

Like me, many entrepreneurs ultimately get where they want to be after a series of failed attempts that range from speed bumps to total blowouts. But rather than park the car entirely, they pull off to the side of the road, fix the problem, and get back on their way. You will face challenges as well. You can, however, make it a little easier on yourself if you reduce the number of rejections you will face, apply the learning to each new endeavor, persevere when the project looks promising, and have the good sense to walk away when it does not.

Reduce the Number of Rejections You Will Face

I would guess that for every product I successfully get licensed, I leave empty-handed on about five others. And on average, I probably pitch each licensed product 6 to 10 times before finally finding a company who wants it. When raising money for a business, the hit rate is even lower.

Success in my business requires persistence and the understanding that rejection is part of the process. It is unreasonable to expect that each product I take on will be a perfect match for one of my clients. But I continue to pitch new ideas all the time because the small percentage of products I do license become quite profitable, making all the other attempts worth the effort. I have learned, however, to be strategic in pitching ideas. Not only does this save time, but it reduces the number of rejections I will face as well as limits the errant feedback I might receive.

When to Pitch

Here is some fatherly advice I plan to give my son in a few years: Do not ask a girl to the prom unless you know the answer is going to be yes. If you are not sure, lower the stakes a little and see if she would like to go to the library and study with you instead. If she says no to the not-really-a-date invitation, then you pretty much know how the stretch limo proposition is going to end.

I give the same advice in business. Do not ask people right away to buy your product or sign up for your newsletter. Instead, court them a little. Tell them you would like their opinion on something you have been working on. The setup is less intimidating and the likelihood of rejection is reduced. By the time you do get around to asking that yes-or-no question, you will already have a sense of what the answer is going to be.

Of course, it is much easier to take the investigative approach if you have not already bought the prom tickets, rented the tuxedo, and paid for the limo. A rejection at that point costs real money and could lead to embarrassment. Again, the same is true in business. Unless you start small with experimental steps, adapting to feedback and only moving forward as the market proves itself interested, you are setting yourself up for an inability (or unwillingness) to change course if the response is negative. At the same time, there comes a point when you do need to ask for the order—hemming and hawing too long will put you in the "He is just a friend" category forever.

Whom to Pitch

When we do BIG Roadshows, we might see 10 concepts out of 100 pitches that have real merit. But just a good idea is not enough for me to get involved with the project. I need to believe we have a good chance of licensing the product as well, so I look for products within my company's areas of strength. That criterion winnows the acceptable ideas down even further than the 10 I originally liked.

If you walk into one of my Roadshows with a great new military device, I will pass on it no matter how impressive it is because we do not work in that industry. Similarly, I often talk to inventors who want me to pitch their products to clients that are not an exact fit, like selling a new hockey mask to a bicycle manufacturer. They tell me the company does not already make or sell hockey equipment of any sort, but they might want to once they see this new invention. While possible, that is not likely to happen. If a product is not a fit, then it cannot be crammed in somewhere no matter how hard you try. So pick the right people before you even try your pitch.

If you ask the buyer at Barbeques Galore whether he would be interested in your new soap dish, the answer is likely to be no. If you ask the same buyer how much you should charge for the product, the answer is likely to be misleading. You need to get out in front of the people who will be your customers. And that can be scary. If enough of them reject your idea, it might mean the idea is not that great after all. But it is better to find out before you invest more heavily in the project so you can either improve the idea or apply the lessons learned to your next great idea. And you *will* have other great ideas.

THINGS YOU SHOULD HAVE SAID

You will not be able to predict everything. But the more prepared you are, the less likely you are to leave a meeting or hang up the phone with regrets over what you should have said. Here are some things you can be prepared to say in order to overcome early objections:

- *Can you give me some feedback?* Do not start off with, "Do you love it?" Instead, ask for advice. Ask for feedback. Ask if you are on the right track and under what circumstances the person might be interested in your product, service, or expertise. You are on a mission to get insight and opinions, not close a deal.

- *That is a good suggestion.* You do not have to take every suggestion offered, but be receptive and go into the meeting with the goal of pulling information rather than pushing your idea. I cannot tell you how often I give advice to inventors who respond immediately with 15 excuses as to why the suggestion will not work, instead of spending just 15 seconds contemplating why it might. Opportunity missed.

- *I do not know.* "I don't know" is a perfectly acceptable response. Just be sure to follow up with a promise to look into the situation and get back to the person with an answer as soon as possible. ("That's a really good question. Let me look into that and call you tomorrow with an answer.")

- Yes. Yes, I can deliver on time. Yes, I can make changes if you need me to. Yes, I can be available by cell phone. Yes, I can teach that class. Yes, I can give you a sample to test. Do not lie to people, but try to be as accommodating as possible when you are just starting out.

    A software trainer, in the early days of her business, answered affirmatively to any class request she received. Then she would go learn the software and develop materials so that by the time the class started, she really could teach it. Over time, she could be selective in teaching only classes she already had training materials for. But when she was first starting out, gaining clients took precedence over minimizing preparation time. You should do the same. In the beginning, you may need to give something away for free in order to overcome early objections and get those first, critical clients to give your ideas a try.

How to Pitch

One of the real tricks in business is figuring out how to establish a relationship. Everyone is already busy and, most of the time, their reaction to something new is similar to how you feel when the phone rings at dinnertime: "Oh great, now what?" You can overcome this reticence and reduce the chances of getting rejected, however, if you give something away for free. I doubt my wife ever would have tried the Tide Laundry Stick had she not gotten a coupon in the mail. But she tried it, loved it, and now buys it at the store herself. Tide managed to get her to try something new because they gave it to her for less than she normally would have to pay. No matter where you are in the development process, find a way to be a giver rather than a taker.

If you are selling birthday cakes, for example, you might give away a free taste. If you are selling a new hand cream, hand out free samples or let people try it out for a week before they have to commit to buying it. If you want to develop a licensing relationship with a large company, offer to give them a summary of the industry research you conducted. If you want kids to take your virtual banjo lessons, let them take one session for free. If you want people to sign up for your cooking newsletter, give them five free recipes as a reward.

Giving almost always results in getting something more valuable back, because either you build a relationship and convert people to paying customers or you find that nobody sticks around after the free stuff is gone and your project needs more tweaking in order to be sustainable.

Where to Pitch

Building a relationship often requires meeting in person. Try to have important meetings face-to-face. So much of our brainwork is the result of perceptions we do not even register—looking someone in the eye, sharing a laugh, discovering a common interest, and so forth. But meeting in person can also be expensive and time-consuming.

The next-best option is the increasingly popular videoconference, because you are virtually face-to-face and still get the benefit of some visual cues. But not everybody has the setup needed to take advantage of this mode. Most everybody, however, does have a telephone, and that is the third-best way to communicate. The telephone is still personal, interactive, convenient, and relatively inexpensive.

There is a big drop in effectiveness as we go from the telephone to mail or e-mail. While both are important tools for moving a project along, they are lousy for relationship building. Although it can be tempting to use standard or electronic mail, hoping to save yourself the awkwardness of getting turned down in person or stumbling through a pitch, you actually increase your chances of rejection using these communication methods. Both modes are easy to disregard or misinterpret. Neither is interactive and comments are easily taken out of context. And besides that, you have no idea whether the person you are trying to reach ever got your message in the first place.

Never do anything important in business via mail or e-mail. Go in person if you can; pick up the phone if you cannot. Use the impersonal alternatives as a last possible resort.

Take the Opportunity to Learn

One of the reasons I believe in pitching people face-to-face as much as possible is because it is very hard to learn from rejection if you cannot get information about why you were turned down. People are more likely to give you that feedback if you are standing there in person or are on the telephone. Mail is the worst, e-mail is only slightly better. When people submit product ideas to BIG, for example, they can come into my office, attend a Roadshow at locations across the country, schedule a conference call, or simply mail in their ideas. Because of the volume we receive, it is very hard for me to give feedback on those items that come in the mail. But if I am talking to someone in person or on the phone during a scheduled session, I will be as helpful as I can in the time I have available. Helpful, however, does not mean I will pretend to like their ideas just to spare their feelings.

I think it is better to reject bad ideas so people will move on to good ones rather than continuing to waste time and money on ideas that stink. Some people listen to my opinion and react professionally while others get defensive, take the critique personally, and think I am a jerk. Those who listen, however, either find ways to overcome the challenges I mention or use the information gained to formulate better ideas in the future.

For example, new inventors often overlook retailer needs. They think of the consumer ("Everybody will love this!") and the manufacturer ("It can be made for pennies!"), but they fail to think about the needs of the middleman who often controls whether or not the public will ever see the product. A frequently overlooked retailer requirement is maximum use of shelf space. So if you bring me a product that measures 2 by 3 feet and sells for $1.99, I will probably tell you there is a problem. A store buyer is unlikely to give up that much shelf space to make just a couple of bucks when he could put five different products that sell for over five dollars each into that same area. Savvy inventors will take that insight and either look for ways to repackage their product into a smaller box or remember to consider footprint size on all future ideas. Disenchanted inventors or those unwilling to consider changes to their product ignore my comments and miss the opportunity to learn and to become more successful product developers.

As you approach people with your products, services, or everyday expertise, try to keep an open mind so you, too, can learn from the experience. Many times I reject products, not because they are bad products, but because they are not a match for my company's needs. That will often be the case with you as well. So do not take it personally when someone says no. Instead, ask for insight and information as to why the person turned you down so you can look for ways to improve your odds of hearing yes the next time.

FOUR QUESTIONS TO ASK
AFTER HEARING THE WORD *NO*

Ah, that crushing blow. You were so hoping to get an affirmative response but got the whammy instead. Do not stomp off in a huff. Now is the perfect opportunity to establish a relationship and get some insight as to why you struck out and how you might be able to work together in the future. Try asking these questions:

1. *If this were your business or your idea, what would you do to change it?* Then get out a pen and paper and be open to what you hear. You might learn ways to improve the current idea, or you might come up with something entirely new just by listening.

2. *Who do you think this is perfect for?* (And can I get their name and number from you?) Remember, a rejection does not necessarily mean your product or service is no good.

It is just not good for that situation. Maybe you can get a referral for a better fit.

3. *What are you looking for?* This is the question that led to the BIG Hunts. We ask it of our clients all the time. I know several independent inventors who have used this same technique as well to establish great relation-ships with clients on their own. Often the product they end up selling or licensing to the company is not the one the inventor called about in the first place.

4. *Thank you for your time and honest feedback.* Sometimes no just means no. So save yourself the argument, and work to build a relationship instead. Think about how much easier it will be to pick up the phone a couple of months from now when you have another great idea that fits the requirements you have been given, and you already know the person you are going to call.

Know When to Walk Away

Sometimes you need to walk away from a project. That, too, can take courage because, at one point, you probably thought you were in the beginning stages of developing your million-dollar idea. But now it is turning out to be a bust instead. Learning from the experience and applying that knowledge toward your next project is the best way to salvage the time and energy spent.

I am a huge advocate of persistence, of course. If you pack it in at every bump in the road, you will never get where you need to go. But if, time after time, your product is turned down, your target demographic visits your web site without buying anything, people unsubscribe from your newsletter, and so forth, it might be time to rethink your strategy. If you have incorporated as many suggestions as possible and success is still not on the horizon, then it is definitely time to be realistic and think about doing something else. When you do finally hit that magic combination where the public reacts favorably to what it is you are offering, you will see that every positive and negative experience leading up to your success happened for your benefit.

As you embark on that quest, think big but start small. View the journey as an experiment and be willing to change directions as you learn more about yourself and the proposed project. If you do have positive response from people, then work to promote the heck out of it and sell your product, service, or everyday expertise to as many people as you can. If, however, the responses are still lukewarm after you already tried to incorporate feedback and adapt to consumer needs as best you can, have the big-picture knowledge necessary to stop the effort, go back to the personal inventory, and try something else instead. I have done this myself many times. And though not every project has turned out as planned, they all have been worth the effort.

OTHER EXPERTS ON REJECTION AND PERSEVERANCE

Joan Airey, Freelance Writer and Stock Photographer*

After I had written an article on request from a magazine, the editor changed her mind on the story angle and asked for a complete rewrite. Frustrated at the time wasted on the first article, I decided to submit it to other magazines. Remembering that another editor had once told me that articles are worth twice as much if submitted with relevant photographs, I took a few pictures and sent them along with the query. The new magazine bought both the article and the pictures. No matter what you are doing, stick with it, give it your best effort, and listen to the advice of other experts. By listening to

*Freelance writer Joan Airey read an article about microstock photography that piqued her interest. So she researched it further and decided to submit pictures of her own. Airey makes as much money with her photography as she does with her writing.

the editor who told me to send pictures with my queries, I have been able to increase my income significantly.

Adena Surabian, Creator of Nature's Baby Organics[*]

Rejection actually helped my business. I had created a wonderful product that I believed every mother would love, so I could not understand why buyers were not placing orders. It took me some time to realize that Nature's Baby Organics were not necessarily a fit for every store I called. Getting feedback from buyers who did not place orders helped me narrow and define my market niche. Once we truly understood our customer needs, we redesigned the packaging and reformulated the products based on their input. Suddenly the products were selling off the shelves, editors were acknowledging our queries, and buyers were calling us for orders.

[*]Adena Surabian became an everyday expert in natural and organic skin care for children when her then one-year-old broke out in a mysterious rash. Unable to find the source, Surabian started investigating all the products her daughter came in contact with. Although she ultimately discovered her daughter is allergic to a chemical commonly found in sunscreen, she suddenly knew too much about the other products in her cupboard to continue using them. Thus began her quest to find and ultimately create more natural alternatives. Nature's Baby Organics can be found at www.naturesbabyproducts.com.

PART FOUR

TOOLS, TIPS, AND TRICKS

Resources for Launching Your Million-Dollar Idea

Ten Tips for Getting Your Business Started Inexpensively

Do not fall into the "It takes money to make money" trap. While there is some degree of truth to that statement, spend as little money as possible until you know for certain that you have the skills and interest needed to sustain your idea. Here are 10 ways to help you do that:

1. Although many of your business expenses can be written off at tax time, do not start loading up the cart at Costco with things you do not really need. You still have to pull money out of your pocket in order to buy that stuff now, and you might not be able to write off as much as you think later. Go to the IRS web site (www.irs.gov) and download Publication 587, entitled "Business Use of Your Home," to learn more.

2. Image is important, but substance is more important. Too many entrepreneurs get so excited about starting a business of their own that they quickly run out and buy a fancy desk, rent office space, and get a new company car, just to project an image of success. What they should be doing is making sales calls, writing web content, and doing other things that will really make an impression. I started my current business using a door stretched across two file cabinets from Home

Depot. I upgraded to a real desk and a nice office space only after the business became profitable.

3. Rather than invest in expensive printed materials such as letterhead, business cards, brochures, and so forth, put your money into a good all-in-one printer that prints, scans, faxes, and copies. Printers and papers available at office supply stores are of very good quality these days, certainly good enough to make your business look professional. Printing your marketing materials as needed also enables you to make changes as the business grows. The last thing you want is 500 full-color brochures that have the wrong cell phone number because you changed services or the wrong pricing information because you learned you could charge more.

   If you still want a professional print job, VistaPrint (www.vistaprint.com) can provide almost anything you need inexpensively. Overnight Prints (www.overnightprints.com) is another option.

4. Many of the forms needed to run a business can be found for free on Microsoft.com. Use those instead of buying pre-printed forms. If you have access to Microsoft Office Publisher (part of the Office tool suite), you can use it to make brochures and newsletters quickly and easily. This software is easy to learn and makes plopping pictures in the middle of text a hundred times easier than doing the same thing using word processing software.

5. Refrain from hiring employees for as long as you can. If you need help, hire contractors instead. But always start with a small assignment to see if the person is capable of delivering what you need. Local colleges are great resources for this. Professors have many contacts and often can refer you to graduate students who will pitch in some free work in the pursuit of class credits. This is an especially good way to get help in Web development, industrial design, or prototyping. If you want a professional with industry experience, put an ad on Craigslist (www.craigslist .com) or try a service like Guru (www.guru.com).

6. Another way to obtain services is to barter with someone, saving both of you from having to pay cash for the help you need. But bartering only works if both parties feel that they gained as much as they gave. To ensure this happens, calculate how much you would charge a cash-paying customer for the same services, and have your friend do the same. Then be sure to arrive at a fair agreement before getting started. A Web developer who charges $1,500 to develop a web site should expect to receive $1,500 worth of services from the person he is bartering with—whether that is a year's worth of lawn care from someone who runs a landscaping service or a day's worth of work from an attorney.

7. One of the best ways to learn about an industry for free is to read popular message boards in online communities devoted to a particular subject. If you want to learn more about wedding planning, for example, research The Knot (www.theknot.-com). If you want to learn more about search engine placement and advertising, check out the forums on Digital Point (http://forums.digitalpoint.com) and Site Point (www.sitepoint.com).

8. Another great way to learn about an industry is to attend trade shows. But attending in person may also mean incurring travel expenses. Most tradeshows put a list of exhibitors on their web site. Rather than physically visiting each booth at the show, you can click through to the various exhibitor web sites from home. The experience may not be as interactive, but it is certainly cheaper.

   To find trade shows, ask different retailers or professionals in the industry for referrals. Or you can consult the Trade Show News Network web site (www.tsnn.com), though the list is not exhaustive.

9. Ask other people how they have done things. People are surprisingly willing to give resources and insight if you are respectful of their time. However, do not ask for a half-day seminar or to be given a template of everything they have done. Ask specific questions after you have done your own homework, such as, "Did you file for a provisional patent or

go straight to a utility patent?" or "Did you hire a service to get search engine optimization, and if so, which one?"

10. Learn how to search the Internet. Virtually everything you need to know is there if you know how to find it. Most search engines have some helpful searching tips on their web sites. On Google, for example, the Support page (www.google.com/support) has a variety of documents to help you navigate the 'Net.

Inexpensive Ways to Get Your Business Online

We have talked a great deal about needing to have an online presence so people can find you, explore what it is you have to offer, and really start to see you for the everyday expert that you are. But setting up a web site can be overwhelming because there are so many different choices available, each ranging in complexity and cost. And the terminology alone—*domain names, web hosting, e-commerce, merchant accounts*, and so forth—is enough to make you wave the white flag.

Although this is not a how-to book, nor is this section an exhaustive resource of Internet basics, I want to give you a push in the right direction by explaining some terminology you might need to know, as well as give you examples of the types of services you might need. I have also included a few tips for hiring a Web developer in case the inability to get started on your own is preventing you from getting started at all.

Terminology

To set up a web site, you need a *domain name* and a *web hosting service*. If you plan to sell stuff online, then you also need an *e-commerce* solution. Let me break that down for you a bit.

Domain Name

The domain name is your web site address. My company's domain name, for example, is www.bigideagroup.net. A domain name that is easy to pronounce, spell, and remember can be a real asset to your business. Before settling on a domain name, however, practice saying it out loud to see if people understand what you are saying. Then ask them what type of business they would expect to find at that web site address. Names some of the everyday experts in this book have selected such as www.cheapdateshow.com and www.hospitalgowns.com, for example, are easy to say and relatively easy to understand. A web site that mixes letters and numbers or has made-up words in it is always going to take a little more energy to explain than one that is simple and straightforward.

Why do you need to know this? Because if you want a completely customized domain name for your web site address, then you need to use a service that gives you that option. If, for example, you sign up for a free blogging web site on WordPress, your free domain name will have "wordpress" in the address: www.yourname. wordpress.com. But for a relatively inexpensive upgrade, you can have a custom domain name without the "wordpress" verbiage: www.yourname.com. I think the custom domain name is worth the few bucks it costs.

Web Hosting

Web hosting is another ominous term that is pretty simple to understand. Basically, when you create a web site from scratch, you end up with a series of pages, graphics, pictures, and so forth. That collection of files needs to be uploaded and stored (hosted) on a computer that is mapped to the Internet for all the world to see.

Why do you need to know this? If you hire a Web developer to build a custom web site, then you need to pay for Web hosting services as well. If you use a template service like Google Page Creator (www.pages.google.com), then the Web hosting service is already part of the package. Places like MySpace also host your Web page, but the service is so fundamental to their business that you do not really even notice it is a feature.

E-Commerce

E-commerce simply refers to the ability to sell things on your web site. Most e-commerce solutions include a shopping cart function (a way for people to select the things they want to buy), credit card processing (a way to pay by credit card), and a merchant account (a bank account the credit card company will deposit your money into when the transaction is approved).

Why do you need to know this? If you build a custom site, you will either have to put these services together on your own or take advantage of one of the many total e-commerce solutions on the market. PayPal (www.paypal.com) is a good example of this. And with Yahoo! Small Business (www.smallbusiness.yahoo.com), you can use templates to create a basic web site and upgrade your service to add e-commerce fairly easily.

Another option is to set up an eBay Store (www.ebay.com) or an Amazon WebStore (www.amazon.com) to sell your products online without having to set up an e-commerce site of your own.

Where to Start

In the early days of the Internet, you had to put all of these pieces together in order to build an online business, and you typically had to pay service fees for each component. You could easily spend a couple hundred dollars a month keeping a basic e-commerce site up and running. But thankfully, several service providers have streamlined the process and now there are many places to set up a domain name, get Web hosting, and add e-commerce if you want. Here are a few resources to check out:

- On Go Daddy (www.godaddy.com), you can buy all the pieces separately and hire a Web designer to create a custom site for you. Or, you can use one of several "Site Builders" the company provides to do the work yourself.

- Google Page Creator (www.pages.google.com) gives you a domain name and web hosting services for free, but your domain name will have "googlepages" in the address (www.yourname

.googlepages.com) unless you pay for an upgrade to have your own custom domain name. Google offers several layout templates and is easy to use.

- Yahoo! also offers free personal web sites with "geocities" in the domain name. But you can upgrade using its Small Business service to get more customized and to have your own domain name as well. See www.smallbusiness.yahoo.com for an online demonstration.

- Try WordPress (www.wordpress.com) or Blogger (www.blogger .com) if you want to set up a free blogging web site. Try TypePad (www.typepad.com) to get a few more customization options. All three services have free trial options so you can test the services before committing.

- Automattic (www.automattic.com), the parent company of WordPress, has a list of web design and software development firms on their web site that you can hire to help you get started. The best way to find this list of WordPress consultants is to select "Services" from the Automattic home page.

- Social networking sites like MySpace (www.myspace.com), YouTube (www.youtube.com), and Squidoo (www.squidoo .com) can also be used to create an online presence. They are not ideal, frankly, but are inexpensive starting places. And although your actual domain name could be lengthy (www .myspace.com/yourname), you can shortcut the address by simply saying, "Look up (yourname) on MySpace." Most people understand how to do that.

Getting Help

Although web site services and Web development software have gotten quite user-friendly, not everybody feels comfortable using these tools. Technology can be mastered with a little time and effort, but it can also be a source of frustration and lack of progress. If that is the case for you, then go ahead and get help. But be sure to plan your site and look for inexpensive developers to save time and money.

Plan Your Site

Do not start with a blank page. When you first meet with a Web developer, come prepared with sample web sites you like, features you need, and a draft of the content for each page. This will help the developer meet your needs quickly and efficiently. Complete the following steps in order to be prepared.

- Look on the Internet for web sites that have a similar look and feel to what you would like to create. Pay attention to all design elements including colors, fonts, layout, and navigation (how you move around the site).

- With three or four example sites in mind, plan the details of your own web site. Think about the features you want, the information you need to put on each page, and how much time you want to invest in keeping the site current after it has been built.

- Start developing the content. Write the information you want to include on the home page, the product or services pages, the "About Us" story, and so forth. A common mistake people make in hiring a web site developer is thinking that the developer is capable of writing the text. That information has to come from you, and if you do not have the text ready when the site is designed, not only will it cause delays but it could lead to a re-design once you figure out what needs to be said.

Find a Developer

The cost of building a web site is a little like getting automotive work done. One shop will charge you $500 to put in new brakes and another shop down the street will charge you $1,500 to do the same job. In looking for a Web developer, ask around until you find a low-priced alternative that comes highly recommended.

- Custom-built web sites typically have a "created by" or "powered by" link on the bottom of the home page that will refer you to the designer who did the work. If you find a site you like, ask the designer how much it would cost to build a similar site for you.

- If that estimate is outside of your getting-started price range, see if you can find a lower-priced designer on Craigslist (www.craigslist.com) or by asking friends and associates for references.

- Colleges are also great resources for this type of work because design students are always looking for ways to get clients for class projects or to make their portfolios look more impressive.

- Social networking sites also have power users and lists of popular pages. On Squidoo, for example, you can see several heavily populated sites from people clearly versed in the technology and often dabbling in more than one social network. You could contact those people to see if they are using a service or are interested in doing some freelance work to help get you started.

Like everything else we talk about in this book, your web site can evolve as well. Start with a good foundation like a domain name that is easy to remember and a template web site that can be set up inexpensively. Then add features and customization as the business grows.

Helpful Web Sites

The problem with publishing a list of web sites in a book is that by the time the book comes out, new resources will be available and others will have disappeared. For that reason, I suggest you use the lists in this chapter as a point in the right direction. When you need help in a particular area, research the web sites I have listed, ask other entrepreneurs for references and referrals, or do some online searching for yourself.

Blog Notes

- A wealth of blog information can be found on Lorelle VanFossen's blog at WordPress (www.lorelle.wordpress.com). She also has a book out called *Blogging Tips: What Bloggers Won't Tell You about Blogging.*

- Technorati (www.technorati.com) lists nearly every blog on the Web. This is a great place to research blogs, see what other people are doing, and find examples of the type of blog you would like to create.

- The Blog Squad (www.blogsquad.biz) has tips and tricks for not only creating a blog but using it as a sales and marketing tool as well.

- If you are looking to add content quickly to your blog, a good tool to use is Clipmarks (www.clipmarks.com). This browser add-on feature allows you to clip online articles, pictures, and videos from another web site and save it to your computer, add it to your blog, e-mail it, or print it. The format is clean and you just clip the section you want. In addition, individuals can share what they have clipped with the Clipmarks community. EzineArticles (www.ezinearticles.com) can be a resource for you as well.

Business in General

- SCORE ("Counselors to America's Small Business") offers free business advice on a range of topics. You can also take classes, schedule one-on-one counseling, and find mentors in your area, all of whom have had successful businesses and are now volunteering their time in order to help others. The SCORE web site (www.score.org) also contains hundreds of useful how-to articles and business tools.

- Finding good printing services is fairly easy these days. VistaPrint (www.vistaprint.com), Overnight Prints (www.overnightprints .com), Staples (www.staples.com), FedEx Kinkos (www.fedex .com), and a variety of other places can print a range of materials inexpensively.

- Avery products (www.avery.com) are particularly good for printing your own materials such as business cards, letterhead, and so forth. The paper is thick and the edges are smooth. Avery's Clean Edge Business Cards, for example, are good enough to pass off as professionally printed cards.

- Save shipping costs by using the U.S. Post Office Priority Mail (www.usps.com) service when you want to ship something quickly. Not only are the prices cheaper than some of the other well-known courier brands, but the mailman will pick up your packages when he delivers the regular mail to your home—saving you time and gas money. If you print and pay for the shipping label online, then the tracking service is free.

Contests

- My firm, Big Idea Group, is constantly running contests. Check us out at www.bigideagroup.net.
- You can learn more about the Henkel Innovation Trophy contest at www.henkel.com.
- See past Staples Invention Quest winners and stay tuned for the next contest at www.staples.com/IQ.
- Cooking Contest Central regularly publishes cooking contests and has an active forum of past winners and future hopefuls. That web site is www.contestcooking.com.
- Invention contests are often announced in *Inventors Digest* (www.inventorsdigest.com), on the United Inventors Association web site (www.uiausa.com), and in other invention forums like Inventor Spot (www.inventorspot.com).

Creative Outlets

- The ongoing T-shirt design competition is at Threadless (www.threadless.com). If you do not want to compete with others and just want a chance to sell your slogans and artwork, try Zazzle instead (www.zazzle.com).
- There are several microstock photography sites. Some of the more popular ones are Can Stock Photo (www.canstockphoto

.com), Shutterstock (www.shutterstock.com) and iStockphoto (www.istockphoto.com).

- Learn about self-publishing on BookLocker.com (www.booklocker.com). Other print-on-demand services include Amazon (www.amazon.com), CafePress (www.cafepress.com), and Greeting Card Universe (www.greetingcarduniverse.com).

- TalentSpeaks (www.talentspeaks.com) is a community for designers and other creative people.

- OurStage (www.ourstage.com) is an online talent community where fans vote for the best artists. Winners receive cash, recognition, and sometimes even mentoring from people inside the elusive entertainment industry.

Industry News

- Use Google Alerts to keep track of what is going on in your industry. To set a Google Alert, go to www.google.com and either sign up for a new account or log in to your existing one. Then go to "My Account" and select "Alerts" from the submenu.

- Find the web site of industry trade shows and magazines online. The Trade Show News Network (www.tsnn.com) and Google Directory (www.directory.google.com) are both good resources. But you can also just ask other professionals in the industry if there are tradeshows, trade journals, or other resources they recommend.

- The Springspotter Network (www.springspotters.com) newsletter sends out reviews and reports of new business ideas and trends in the market.

Inventing and Product Development

User Forums

- Although IPWatchdog.com is primarily geared toward inventing, the web site is full of other business advice as well. It has some great free sample confidentiality agreements that are easy to understand as well as a load of information on everything from patents and copyrights to why linking to other web sites will increase your own search engine ranking.

- Inventor Spot (www.inventorspot.com) is another good resource.

- The United Inventors Association (www.uiausa.org) can help you find an inventor group in your area.

- *Inventors Digest* (www.inventorsdigest.com) is the only magazine geared solely towards inventing. *Entrepreneur* (www.entrepreneur.com) is also a good resource because it talks both about inventing and business innovations.

- Barbara Russell Pitts and her sister Mary Russell Sarao write a regular column for *Inventors Digest* and have written a book full of money-saving tips called *Inventing on a Shoestring Budget*. Their web site, Ask the Inventors (www.asktheinventors.com), is another great resource.

Prototyping

- McMaster-Carr Supply Company (www.mcmaster.com) has every part imaginable. If you do not find the piece you are looking for, you can probably find something to hack apart or two things to glue together in order to create a mock-up of what you need.

- eMachineShop.com (www.emachineshop.com) is another good resource for getting a reasonably priced prototype.

- Ponoko (www.ponoko.com) will not work for every type of product, but appears to be a good place for testing out inventions that can be die-cut.

- Shapelock (www.shapelock.com) provides reusable heat-and-mold plastic pellets that you can shape into the parts and pieces you need to test your theories.

Legal Resources

- The U.S. Patent and Trademark Office (www.uspto.gov) lists all existing patents and applications older than 18 months old.

Start here whenever you have a new idea to be sure it does not already exist.

- Get free legal advice on Nolo (www.nolo.com) and find inexpensive legal documents on Legal Zoom (www.legalzoom .com).

Other

- Stephen Key's inventRight seminars (www.inventright.com) are fun and enlightening. Key is a successful inventor who has both licensed products and sold them on his own.
- Don Debelak (www.dondebelak.com) also has an informative web site for entrepreneurs and inventors. Debelak is the author of several invention books and the author of a regular column in *Entrepreneur* magazine.

Places to Sell Your Stuff

- You can sell your services and merchandise on Craigslist (www.craigslist.com), MyPlace2Sell (www.myplace2sell.com), eBay (www.ebay.com), and Amazon.com (www.amazon.com).
- Sell homemade items on Etsy (www.etsy.com).
- Sell music on CD Baby (www.cdbaby.com).

Podcast Sites

- Learn more about podcasting and listen to what others are doing on PodCast Pickle (www.podcastpickle.com), Podcast .net (www.podcast.net), Podcast Alley (www.podcastalley .com), and iTunes (www.apple.com/itunes/store/podcasts.html).

Publicity and Promotion

- For artists, designers, and other everyday experts who want to send quick visuals of their work to prospective clients, Modern Postcard (www.modernpostcard.com) is a great resource. Shannon Kaye, decorative painter, used this service to send out a postcard highlighting one of her recent projects about every six months to designers, architects, and others who might be interested in her work. After a few different cards arrived in the mail, people began to pay attention to Kaye's creativity and versatility. One postcard even led to some freelance work for the Pottery Barn Kids catalog.

- I cannot say enough about Joan Stewart's Publicity Hound web site (www.publicityhound.com). She has a wealth of information on how to write press releases and pitch the media. Bill Stroller's Publicity Insider web site (www.publicityinsider .com) is also worth exploring.

- Submit press releases online to all the major media outlets through PRWeb (www.prweb.com) or PR Newswire (www .prnewswire.com).

- Write free articles to position yourself as an expert and post them on EzineArticles (www.ezinearticles.com).

- Networking sites like Facebook (www.facebook.com), Meetup (www.meetup.com), and LinkedIn (www.linkedin.com) can help you connect with other people in your industry or reconnect with people you share common interests or experiences with, such as where you went to high school or college, or where you worked.

Miscellaneous

- At Jigsaw (www.jigsaw.com) you can find contact information for several people including media players like producers for daytime television talk shows. You can get free information by providing contact information on the people in your network or you can pay a low monthly fee to just get the contact information you need.

- If you do not understand a term or a concept, start with Wikipedia (www.wikipedia.org). Not only can you learn enough to get started, but most Wikipedia pages also have a list of resources and links to explore.

- About.com (www.about.com) covers hundreds of topics and has a great deal of user-friendly information to boost your expertise on nearly any subject.

- We have talked about Helium (www.helium.com) and Squidoo (www.squidoo.com) as ways to establish a web site and publish your expertise. But both sites are also good resources for learning. On Squidoo, for example, there are a couple different sites with good how-to information on uploading videos to the Web.

Web Traffic and Ad Revenue

- SitePoint (www.sitepoint.com) and the forums at Digital Point (http://forums.digitalpoint.com) are good resources for learning about search engine optimization (SEO).

- Use Google AdSense (www.google.com/adsense) to make money through advertising on your site.

Everyday Experts Roll Call

I want to thank all of the everyday experts featured in this book who willingly shared their stories and insights in order to help others achieve success. I encourage you to check out their web sites, where applicable, listed here, and look for ways in which you can emulate their success.

Joan Airey, freelance writer and photographer

Stephanie Allen and Tina Kuna, Dream Dinners
www.dreamdinners.com

Paige Snear Apar and Vanessa McGarry, inventors

Kim Babjak, inventor
www.kimcoaz.com

Todd Basche, Wordlock
www.wordlock.com

Roger Brown, inventor
www.rogerbrown.net

Lee Carlson, Dull Men's Club
  www.dullmen.com

Keith Carter, illustrator
  www.kcarterart.blogspot.com

Steve Collins, high school basketball coach in case study

Jennifer Cosgrove, greeting card artist
  www.gcuniverse.com/jencosgrove

David Crawford, songwriter
  http://davidcrawford.fuzz.com

Laura Cunitz, Bella Knitting
  www.bellaknitting.com

Arra David, product developer and engineer
  www.sea-stones.com

Izzy Dean, Props and Pans
  www.propsandpans.com

Donna DeClemente, DDC Marketing Group
  www.ddcmarketing.com

Sandra Grauschopf, contest guide for About.com
  www.contests.about.com

Ernestine Grindal, Ernestine's Easel
  www.balsamlanestudio.com

Kelly Hales, recipe doctor in case study

Brooke Hall, graphic artist in case study
  www.brookehalldesign.com

Laura Heuer, Jakoter Health Organizers
  www.jakoter.com

Kelley Hill, Hillgirls Music
  www.kelleyhill.com

Kim and Scott Holstein, Kim & Scott's Pretzels
  www.kimandscotts.com

Angela Hoy, WritersWeekly.com
  www.writersweekly.com

Shannon Kaye, decorative painter
www.shannonkaye.com

Susan Kern, inventor

Stephen Key, inventRight and Hot Picks
www.inventright.com
www.hotpicksusa.com

Charles E. Kirk, The Kirk Report
www.thekirkreport.com

Corrie Kuipers, greeting card artist
www.corrieweb.nl

Will Leitch, DeadSpin
www.deadspin.com

Lisa Lillien, Hungry Girl
www.hungry-girl.com

Nick Lindauer, Sweat 'N Spice and Hot Sauce Blog
www.sweatnspice.com
www.hotsauceblog.com.

Joe and Lisa Lynn, *Cheap Dates* podcast
www.cheapdateshow.com

Ben Martino, photographer
www.geocities.com/photographer01440

Kelly A. Mello, journalist
www.helium.com/user/show/58594

Amie O'Shaughnessy, Ciao Bambino
www.ciaobambino.com

Betty Parham, Cooking Contest Central
www.contestcooking.com

Weston Phillips, Five Point Productions
www.5pointproductions.com

Barbara Russell Pitts and Mary Russell Sarao, inventors
www.asktheinventors.com

Angie and David Porter, FURminator Inc.
www.furminator.com

Arthur Russ, Nathanville
www.nathanville.co.uk

Jim Ruth, writer
www.helium.com/user/show/320751

Julie Savage, Ideas to Grow
www.ideastogrow.com

Judy Seegmiller, author of *Life with Big Al (Early Alzheimer's)
A Caregiver's Diary*
www.rbl.net

Clifford Shakun, HospitalGowns.com
www.hospitalgowns.com

Joan Stewart, The Publicity Hound
www.publicityhound.com

Adena Surabian, Nature's Baby Organics
www.naturesbabyproducts.com

Eric Teng, inventor of the Garlic Twist
www.garlictwist.com

Lauren Traub Teton, SnowboardSecrets.com
www.snowboardsecrets.com

Peter Tobin, writer